# EMERIL'S
# KICKED-UP
# SANDWICHES

# ALSO BY EMERIL LAGASSE

# EMERIL'S KICKED-UP SANDWICHES

## STACKED WITH FLAVOR

# Emeril Lagasse

WITH PHOTOGRAPHS BY STEVEN FREEMAN

WILLIAM MORROW
*An Imprint of* HarperCollins*Publishers*

FIRST EDITION

*Designed by Leah Carlson-Stanisic*

Library of Congress Cataloging-in-Publication Data
    Lagasse, Emeril.
    Emeril's kicked-up sandwiches: stacked with flavor / Emeril Lagasse;
  with photography by Steven Freeman.
      p.  cm.
    Includes bibliographical references and index.
    ISBN 978-0-06-174297-2 (pbk.)
    1. Sandwiches.  I. Title.
  TX818.L44 2012
  641.84—dc23                              2012018049

12  13  14  15  16  ID5/RRD  10  9  8  7  6  5  4  3  2

For Hilda and Aldie, with love

# CONTENTS

# ACKNOWLEDGMENTS

When making sandwiches, each and every part is just as important as the other, and when one part is missing it just isn't the same. So it is with everyone below—each of you played a part in helping make this book everything I knew it could be and more:

*My family*—Alden, EJ, Meril, Jessie, Jilly, Mom, Dad, Mark, Wendi, Katti Lynn, Dolores, Jason, Jude, John Peter, and Steven.

*My culinary team:* Charlotte Martory, Alain Joseph, Stacey Meyer, and Kamili Hemphill.

*My Homebase team:* Eric Linquest, Tony Cruz, Dave McCelvey, Marti Dalton, Chef Chris Wilson, Chef Bernard Carmouche, Tony Lott, Scott Farber, Doug Doran, George Ditta, Maggie McCabe, and Jeff Hinson. Plus all of the dedicated employees at Homebase and at each of my restaurants.

*Photographer* Steven Freeman, assistant Kevin Guiler, and prop stylist Jen Lover.

*My Martha Stewart Living Omnimedia associates:* Martha Stewart, Lisa Gersh, Lucinda Scala Quinn, Sarah Carey, and Lesley Levenson.

Michelle Terrebonne and Paige Capossela Green.

*My HarperCollins associates:* Cassie Jones, Jessica McGrady, Liate Stehlik, Lynn Grady, Tavia Kowalchuk, Lauren Cook, Shawn Nicholls, Ann Cahn, Kathie Ness, Leah Carlson-Stanisic, and Karen Lumley.

*My partners:* B&G Foods, Green Mountain Coffee Roasters Inc., Groupe SEB/T-Fal, New Orleans Fish House, Nuovo Pasta, and SED International.

*Friends:* Jim Griffin and Mark Stein.

# INTRODUCTION

### What makes a good sandwich great?

As someone who has spent a fair share of time in restaurant kitchens over the years, I've witnessed some pretty inspired sandwich combinations. Is it the bread? Is it the condiments? Is it what's inside? It's all of the above, of course, and often the best combinations are the result of a happy accident or just using what's available. Just imagine what a restaurant cook can pull together from bits and pieces of this and that from around the stations of the kitchen! Who would have thought that leftover shrimp rémoulade from the salad station would make such a killer addition to a classic BLT? But wait—kick it up one notch further by using a slice of fried green tomato from the appetizer station! The same is true at home: Don't overlook last night's dinner leftovers—they might form the basis of the next sandwich masterpiece! (Case in point: the much-anticipated day-after-Thanksgiving roast turkey sandwich with stuffing and cranberry sauce.) Inspiration is everywhere when it comes to sandwiches, and thinking outside the box when it comes to combinations sometimes pays off with real winners.

### Who doesn't love a good sandwich?

Whether you're talking PB&J on soft white bread or a killer BLT on crisped toast with lots of mayo, for many of us sandwiches are part of a daily ritual that dates back to our childhood—a ritual that is comforting in the most basic way and that is enjoyed by almost every culture around the world. Think Middle Eastern pitas, Latin American tacos and empanadas, or even the lettuce wraps of Korea. But take even the simplest sandwich and dress it up: add a condiment here and there and serve it up on artisanal or homemade bread (or a tortilla or a rice paper wrap!) and you'll find yourself appreciating sandwiches in an entirely new way.

### Dress it up!

A lot of what makes or breaks a sandwich is the condiments. Chefs love tinkering with basic condiments and putting their own spin on mayos and spreads of all sorts, and sandwiches are a great vehicle to showcase just about any kind of sauce or spread you can imagine. Add a simple flavored mayonnaise to a sandwich made of sliced roast chicken on toasted white bread and it's instantly elevated to another realm. Chutneys, jams, salsas, and salad dressings are right at home on sandwiches, too, and are just the beginning of the ideas you'll find in the extensive condiment chapter at the end of this book. It is my hope that you will use the recipes in that chapter not only for the sandwich combinations presented to you here, but also as an inspiration for other kitchen projects. Too much basil in the garden? Add some to a homemade mayonnaise and you have a delicious basil mayo. Not sure what to do with all the peppers from your CSA or farm box? Homemade harissa makes great use of those and is a delightful addition to many dishes. The possibilities are endless. Experiment, mix it up, make them your own.

### Knead bread?

It's all about the bread, baby! Experiment with different textures and types, and if you're up for it, there are just under a dozen recipes for home bread baking beginning on page 271 that will make a baker out of you. Don't underestimate the power of bread baking: it was my first job at a Portuguese bakery, and it cemented my love of cooking and helped me decide to go on to culinary school. There's something magical about watching the combination of flour and water turn into something so elementally satisfying. But if you're short on kitchen time, don't worry. Folks who don't want to bake bread at home are now able to purchase bakery-quality breads in their local supermarkets. I urge you to use the breads you like but also to play around with switching breads and fillings to find out just how much the textural "wrapper" affects the sandwich that ends up on your plate. And, hey, even though the strictest definition of a sandwich probably includes sliced bread, it isn't *always* a player, and I've included a few "sandwiches" here that may stretch the envelope a bit—

such as the Fresh Tuna and Butter Lettuce Wraps on page 194, the calzones on page 181, and the samosas on page 211. But by and large, sandwiches can only be as good as the bread they're served on. It's just that simple.

The years I have spent tinkering with various sandwiches in my kitchen prompted me to explore some seriously outrageous combinations from around the corner and around the world—sandwiches that I hope will make you hungry and inspire you to create your own personal classics.

Eggplant Muffuletta,
see page 27

# KICKED-UP
# CLASSICS

The Reuben and The Rachel,
see pages 3–4

# THE REUBEN

4 sandwiches

Hey, guys, this is so easy to make at home. And just as delicious, if not better, as the one from your favorite shop. The freshly made Thousand Island Dressing is killer, and as long as you continue to build this sandwich with the best of ingredients, you can't lose. The other secret to this sandwich is to griddle, baby, griddle.

½ cup Thousand Island Dressing (page 338)
8 slices rye bread
8 ounces sliced Emmenthaler cheese
1 cup sauerkraut, drained if necessary
1½ pounds thinly sliced corned beef or pastrami
3 tablespoons butter, at room temperature

1. Spread 1 tablespoon of the Thousand Island Dressing on each slice of bread. Divide the cheese, sauerkraut, and pastrami among 4 of the slices, and top each sandwich with the remaining bread. Spread the tops of the sandwiches with half of the butter.

2. Heat a 12-inch (or larger) skillet over medium heat. Add the sandwiches, buttered side down, in batches if necessary, and weight them down with a cast-iron press or another heavy skillet. Cook the sandwiches until golden brown and crisped, 2 to 3 minutes. Butter the top of the sandwiches with the remaining butter, turn them over, and cook them for another 2 to 3 minutes. Transfer the sandwiches to a cutting board, slice them in half, and serve immediately.

# THE RACHEL

4 sandwiches

The Rachel is the Reuben's cousin, made with turkey instead of corned beef or pastrami. This one is even more special, with its homemade Russian Dressing and kicked-up Jicama Coleslaw.

8 slices rye bread
½ cup Russian Dressing (page 336)
8 ounces sliced Swiss cheese
12 ounces sliced roasted turkey breast
1 cup Jicama Coleslaw (page 63)

1. Position an oven rack in the center and preheat the oven to 350°F.

2. Arrange the bread in a single layer on a parchment-lined baking sheet. Spread 2 tablespoons of the Russian dressing on each of 4 bread slices. For each sandwich, layer 2 slices of the cheese on top of the dressing, then layer 3 slices of the turkey on top of the cheese. Transfer the baking sheet to the oven and cook until the bread is slightly toasted, the turkey is warmed, and the cheese is completely melted, about 6 minutes.

3. Remove from the oven and carefully transfer the sandwiches and the toast to a work surface. Divide the slaw evenly among the turkey-topped slices, and then top with the remaining toast. Serve immediately.

# BLT WITH FRIED GREEN TOMATOES AND SHRIMP RÉMOULADE

4 sandwiches

This sandwich was a special on the menu at Emeril's in New Orleans. I love it so much that I just had to share it. It may seem like a lot of work, but trust me, it's worth it. The shrimp and the rémoulade sauce can be prepared a day in advance to take some of the pressure off and then combined just before serving.

### Shrimp

4 quarts water

1 tablespoon liquid crab boil, such as Zatarain's

2 lemons, halved

2 bay leaves

Salt

1 pound medium shrimp, peeled and deveined

About ½ cup Rémoulade Sauce, either Creole (page 335) or French (page 336)

### Fried green tomatoes

1 pound medium green tomatoes

1 teaspoon salt

½ teaspoon freshly ground black pepper

1 cup all-purpose flour

½ teaspoon cayenne pepper

½ cup buttermilk (see Note, page 64)

2 large eggs, beaten

1 cup yellow cornmeal

½ cup vegetable oil, plus more as needed

4 cups chopped romaine lettuce

1 tablespoon extra-virgin olive oil

8 slices Pullman bread or other white sandwich bread
   (see page 303), toasted

8 strips thick-cut applewood-smoked bacon,
   cooked until crisp and cut in half

1. To prepare the shrimp: In a 6-quart saucepan set over high heat, combine the water with 2 teaspoons of the crab boil, the lemons, the bay leaves, and a generous amount of salt (enough to make it taste almost like sea water), and bring to a boil.

2. Prepare an ice bath, and add the remaining 1 teaspoon crab boil to it along with enough salt to make the water taste like the sea.

3. Add the shrimp to the boiling water and cook for 2 to 3 minutes, or until just cooked through. Immediately transfer the shrimp to the ice bath and allow them to cool. As soon as the shrimp are cool enough to handle, chop them into bite-size pieces. Toss the shrimp with enough of the Rémoulade Sauce to coat (about ¼ cup), and refrigerate until you are ready to assemble the sandwiches. (Reserve the remaining Rémoulade Sauce.)

4. To fry the tomatoes: Slice the tomatoes crosswise into ¼-inch-thick slices. Season the tomatoes with ½ teaspoon of the salt and ¼ teaspoon of the pepper. Put the flour in a shallow bowl and season it with the remaining ½ teaspoon salt, ¼ teaspoon pepper, and the cayenne. In another shallow bowl, whisk together the buttermilk and eggs. Put the cornmeal in another shallow bowl. Dredge the tomatoes first in the flour, coating the slices evenly on both sides and tapping off any excess. Dip them in the egg wash and let the excess drip off. Then dredge them in the cornmeal, tapping off any excess. Set aside on a plate.

5. Heat the ½ cup vegetable oil in a large sauté pan over medium heat. Pan-fry several tomato slices in the hot oil until golden brown, about 2 minutes on each side. Drain on paper towels. Add more oil to the pan as necessary to fry the remaining tomato slices.

6. To assemble the sandwiches: In a small bowl, toss the chopped romaine with the extra-virgin olive oil.

7. Lay 4 slices of the toast on a work surface, and top each one with 1 tablespoon of the remaining Rémoulade Sauce. Evenly divide the lettuce among them, top with the fried green tomato slices, and add the bacon. Place ½ cup of the shrimp on top of the bacon, and then top each with a remaining slice of toast. Cut the sandwiches in half and serve immediately.

# FRIED SOFT-SHELL CRAB SANDWICHES WITH LEMON CAPER MAYO

4 sandwiches

When you see fresh soft-shell crabs at your local farmer's market or seafood market, you just have to buy them. They're delicious no matter what you do with them, but I like to batter and deep-fry them and turn them into a sandwich to die for.

Vegetable oil, for deep-frying

1 cup all-purpose flour

2 teaspoons Emeril's Original Essence or Creole Seasoning (recipe follows), plus more for seasoning

½ teaspoon salt

¼ teaspoon cayenne pepper

2 large eggs

2 tablespoons buttermilk (see Note, page 64) or whole milk

4 large soft-shell crabs, cleaned (see Note), rinsed, and patted dry

4 Brioche Buns (page 272) or store-bought brioche, cut in half

4 tablespoons (½ stick) unsalted butter, melted

½ cup Lemon Caper Mayo (page 312)

1 cup shredded Bibb lettuce

1 cup thinly sliced yellow bell pepper

½ cup thinly sliced red onion

1. Preheat the oven to 275°F.

2. Fill a large pot with vegetable oil to a depth of 2 inches, and heat it to 375°F.

3. Combine the flour, Essence, ¼ teaspoon of the salt, and the cayenne in a bowl or plate for dredging.

4. In a small bowl, beat the eggs and buttermilk.

5. One at a time, lightly coat the crabs with the flour mixture, then dip them into the egg wash, and finally coat them with more flour mixture.

6. Brush both halves of the buns with the melted butter, place them on a baking sheet, and heat them in the oven until warm, 4 to 6 minutes.

7. With tongs, lower 2 crabs at a time into the hot oil (be careful—they may spatter and pop). Fry, turning them once, until golden and crisp, 3 to 4 minutes. Drain on paper towels and season lightly with the Essence.

8. Spread 1 tablespoon of the mayonnaise on each half of the buns. Cut each crab in half and stack them on the bottom halves. Add the lettuce, yellow pepper, and red onion, and then set the top halves over the crab. Serve immediately.

Note: To clean soft-shell crabs, rinse them under cold running water and scrub them with a small brush to remove any dirt from their outer shells, if necessary. Twist off and discard the apron. Fold back the pointed sides of the top shell to expose the gills; remove the gills on both sides. Using kitchen scissors, cut across the front of the crab, about ¼ inch behind the eyes and mouth, and squeeze out the small sac hiding directly behind the mouth. The crabs are now ready to be cooked.

## Creole Seasoning

2/3 cup

2½ tablespoons paprika

2 tablespoons salt

2 tablespoons garlic powder

1 tablespoon freshly ground black pepper

1 tablespoon onion powder

1 tablespoon cayenne pepper

1 tablespoon dried oregano

1 tablespoon dried thyme

Combine all the ingredients thoroughly. Store in an airtight container in a cool, dark place for up to 6 months.

# GRILLED FLANK STEAK SANDWICHES WITH BALSAMIC-GLAZED PEPPERS AND PROVOLONE

4 sandwiches

For this sandwich, marinated steak is charred in a grill pan and bell peppers are slow-cooked with onions and finished with balsamic vinegar. Oh, yeah, babe, the peppers are killer. Great on steak, but don't stop there—add them to the simplest sandwich for a big impact.

1½ pounds flank steak

1 cup chopped onion

¾ cup chopped fresh parsley leaves

3 tablespoons chopped garlic

½ cup red wine vinegar

1 tablespoon plus 1 teaspoon freshly squeezed lemon juice

2 teaspoons grated lemon zest

2½ teaspoons freshly ground black pepper, plus more for seasoning

½ teaspoon crushed red pepper

1 cup plus 1 tablespoon olive oil

4 cups sliced mixed red, yellow, and orange bell peppers

1 cup sliced red onion

1 teaspoon kosher salt, plus more for seasoning

1 cup balsamic vinegar

2 teaspoons sugar

4 cups baby arugula, rinsed and spun dry

Extra-virgin olive oil, as needed

4 slices provolone cheese

8 slices sourdough sandwich bread, toasted

Mayonnaise, homemade (see page 309) or store-bought

1. Place the flank steak in a gallon-size resealable plastic bag. In a medium bowl, combine the chopped onion, ½ cup of the parsley, 2 tablespoons of the garlic, the red wine vinegar, lemon juice, lemon zest, 2 teaspoons of the black pepper, and the crushed red pepper. Whisk in the 1 cup of olive oil, and pour the marinade into the bag. Seal the bag and refrigerate for at least 2 hours and up to overnight.

2. Heat the remaining 1 tablespoon olive oil in a large sauté pan over medium-high heat. Add the peppers, red onion, ½ teaspoon of the salt, and the remaining tablespoon of garlic, and reduce the heat to medium-low. Cook the peppers, stirring as needed, until soft, about 20 minutes. Add the balsamic vinegar and sugar to the pan, and cook for 10 minutes more, or until the vinegar is reduced to a syrup and the peppers are well coated. Remove the pan from the heat, stir in the remaining ¼ cup parsley, and set aside to cool.

3. Remove the flank steak from the marinade and pat it dry. Discard the marinade. Season the steak all over with the remaining ½ teaspoon salt and ½ teaspoon black pepper. Heat a grill pan over high heat, and when it is hot, add the steak. Grill the steak for 4 to 5 minutes per side for medium-rare. Remove it from the pan and allow it to rest for at least 5 minutes; then slice it thinly across the grain.

4. Place the arugula in a bowl and lightly dress it with extra-virgin olive oil, salt, and pepper.

5. To assemble: Lay 1 slice of cheese on each of 4 slices of the toast (if desired, warm them in the oven until melted). Spread mayonnaise on the remaining 4 slices of toast. Divide the steak among the cheese-topped toasts, and season lightly with salt and pepper. Mound the peppers over the steak, and then add the arugula. Top the sandwiches with the remaining toast, cut them in half, and serve immediately.

# HORSERADISH-CRUSTED TENDERLOIN WITH CREOLE MUSTARD MAYO

4 sandwiches

This is a really easy steak sandwich—the tenderloin cooks quickly, and you know it's tender. I guess that's why I like it so much. Some of the crust may fall off when you slice into it, but don't despair—scoop it up and sprinkle it over the meat to get that nice horseradish flavor.

1½ pounds center-cut beef tenderloin, trimmed

¼ cup garlic cloves

¼ cup finely chopped shallot

2 tablespoons minced canned anchovies, or 6 whole fillets

1½ teaspoons kosher salt, plus more for seasoning

1 teaspoon freshly ground black pepper, plus more for seasoning

2 tablespoons fresh thyme leaves

¼ cup extra-virgin olive oil

4 ounces fresh horseradish, finely grated (about ½ cup; see Note)

Four 4-inch sections ciabatta bread (about 1½ loaves), halved lengthwise

About ¾ cup Creole Mustard Mayo (page 310)

½ cup ⅛-inch-thick red onion rounds

2 cups fresh arugula, rinsed and spun dry

2 cups fresh spinach, rinsed and spun dry

1 tablespoon sherry vinegar

1. Allow the tenderloin to sit at room temperature for at least 30 minutes and up to 1 hour.

2. Position an oven rack in the center and preheat the oven to 400°F.

3. Place the garlic, shallot, anchovies, ½ teaspoon of the salt, ½ teaspoon of the pepper, and the thyme in a food processor and pulse to blend. With the motor running, add the oil in a steady stream. Transfer the paste to a small mixing bowl. Stir in the horseradish.

4. Season the tenderloin on all sides with the remaining 1 teaspoon salt and ½ teaspoon black pepper, and evenly coat it with the horseradish mixture. Transfer the tenderloin to a small roasting pan and roast until the thickest part registers 130°F (for medium-rare) on an instant-read thermometer, 35 to 40 minutes. Remove it from the oven, tent it with foil, and set it aside to rest for about 20 minutes. Then slice the tenderloin crosswise into ¼-inch-thick slices.

5. Place the bread, cut side up, on a baking sheet. Pinch and remove some of the bread filling, leaving about ½ inch of thickness. Place the baking sheet in the oven and toast until slightly crisp, about 5 minutes. Transfer the toast to a work surface. Spread about 1½ tablespoons of the Creole Mustard Mayonnaise over each piece. Layer 4 to 6 slices of tenderloin on each bottom half of the toast. Divide the onion slices among the sandwiches.

6. Place the arugula and spinach in a mixing bowl. Drizzle the sherry vinegar over the top, and season with a few generous pinches of salt and pepper. Toss to coat well. Divide the greens among the sandwiches, and complete with the top halves. Serve immediately.

> Note: Fresh horseradish can be found at Whole Foods and in many supermarkets.

# EMERIL'S MONTE CRISTO

16 small sandwiches, 4 to 6 servings

Talk about outrageous! This is a battered and deep-fried ham, turkey, and cheese sandwich. Don't be apprehensive about the confectioners' sugar and the preserves. Give this classic combo a try; it'll truly knock your socks off. And let me tell you, I don't even know what it would do to your guests over brunch!

8 slices White Sandwich Bread (page 303)

Whole-grain or Dijon-style mustard

Mayonnaise, homemade (see page 309),
    or store-bought

12 ounces sliced Swiss cheese

8 ounces sliced Black Forest ham

4 ounces sliced cheddar cheese

4 ounces sliced smoked turkey

4 tablespoons (½ stick) butter,
    at room temperature

1¼ cups all-purpose flour

1 teaspoon baking soda

1 teaspoon baking powder

¼ teaspoon salt

One 12-ounce bottle American-style lager,
    such as Budweiser

Vegetable oil, for frying

Confectioners' sugar, for serving

Peach preserves or your favorite fruit preserves, for serving

1. Lay the bread slices on a clean work surface. Evenly spread mustard on 4 slices and mayonnaise on the other 4 slices. Lay a slice of Swiss cheese on each of the mustard slices, tucking it in to fit without hanging over. Top with 2 slices of ham, a slice of cheddar, a slice of turkey, and finally another slice of Swiss cheese, continuing to fold and tuck as you go. Close the sandwiches with the mayonnaise-coated slices of bread. Butter the outsides of the bread. Lightly press the sandwiches, and tightly wrap each one in plastic wrap; refrigerate for at least 30 minutes and up to overnight.

2. In a medium bowl, combine the flour, baking soda, baking powder, and salt. Whisk in the beer and set aside.

3. Fill a small pot with vegetable oil to a depth of about 4 inches, and heat it to 350°F.

4. Unwrap the sandwiches and cut each one into 4 pieces—either squares or triangles, whichever shape you prefer. Using a pair of tongs and working with a few at a time, dip a sandwich section into the beer batter and then lower it into the hot oil. Work carefully and quickly, cooking for about 1 minute until golden and crispy on all sides. Remove the sandwich sections from the oil with a slotted spoon or strainer, and set them aside to drain briefly on paper towels. Dust lightly with confectioners' sugar. Repeat with the remaining sandwiches.

5. Serve the sandwiches immediately, with the preserves served on the side for dipping or spreading, as desired.

# SANDWICH NIÇOISE

4 sandwiches

You read it right: This is salad niçoise layered between pieces of yummy focaccia. Though each component definitely stands on its own, from anchovy-marinated beans to black olive mayo, boy, oh boy, when you put them together . . . be ready! I pepper-crust and sear fresh tuna steaks for a powerful bite, but you can also enjoy this sandwich using very good-quality canned tuna (drained and flaked) instead.

3 tablespoons mixed black, green, and pink peppercorns

Two 1-inch-thick tuna steaks (about 1 pound)

¼ cup canola, grapeseed, or vegetable oil

¼ teaspoon kosher salt

½ cup thinly sliced shallot

Finely grated zest of 1 lemon (about ½ teaspoon)

2 tablespoons freshly squeezed lemon juice

4 to 6 large canned anchovy fillets, minced
    (about 4 teaspoons)

3 tablespoons extra-virgin olive oil

⅛ teaspoon salt

8 ounces haricots verts or green beans

Kalamata Olive Mayo (page 311)

Four 4 x 4-inch pieces focaccia (see page 279),
    split horizontally, or 8 slices other bread,
    trimmed to same size

4 hard-boiled eggs, sliced

8 thin tomato slices, lightly salted

1. Enclose the peppercorns in a resealable plastic food storage bag, and set it on a flat, stable surface. Using a meat mallet or the bottom of a cast-iron skillet, crack the peppercorns until they all are split and no whole peppercorns remain. Oil the tuna steaks with 2 tablespoons of the oil, and coat the tuna on all sides with the cracked pepper. If you are going to cook the tuna right away, season it with the kosher salt. Otherwise wait until you are ready to cook before sprinkling with the salt.

2. Heat the remaining 2 tablespoons oil in a medium sauté pan over high heat. Add the tuna steaks, reduce the heat to medium-high, and sear on one side for 1 minute. Turn the steaks over and sear on the other side, no more than 1 minute for medium-rare. Remove the tuna from the pan and set it aside to cool. Then cover and refrigerate up to overnight before using, if desired. When ready to assemble the sandwiches, cut the tuna into ¼-inch-thick slices.

3. Combine the shallot, lemon zest, lemon juice, and anchovies in a medium bowl. Whisk in the olive oil and add the salt. Set aside.

4. Bring a medium saucepan of lightly salted water to a boil. Fill a medium bowl with ice and cold water. Add the haricots verts to the boiling water and simmer for 3 minutes, or until just tender. Drain the beans and then plunge them into the ice bath. When they have cooled completely, drain well and toss with the vinaigrette.

5. Spread Kalamata Olive Mayo on the top halves of the focaccia pieces. Lay the haricots verts in a row across the bottom halves of the focaccia, being sure to include some shallots and drops of the vinaigrette. Top with the slices of egg and tomato. Lay the tuna slices across the tomato. Place the top halves of the focaccia over the tuna, and serve immediately.

# TURKEY WALDORF SANDWICH

4 sandwiches

Although we do not know for sure, it has been said that the Waldorf salad was created at the Waldorf-Astoria Hotel in 1896. At its core the recipe consists of apples, celery, and mayonnaise. The salad has taken many twists and turns over the years, and this is ours.

One 2½-pound split turkey breast, bone in and skin on
   (see Note)
2¾ teaspoons sea salt or kosher salt
1 teaspoon freshly ground black pepper
¼ cup olive oil
½ cup toasted and chopped pecans
½ cup plus 2 tablespoons plain Greek-style yogurt
¼ cup plus 2 tablespoons mayonnaise,
   homemade (see page 309), or store-bought
1 tablespoon chopped fresh parsley leaves
2 teaspoons cider vinegar
1 Honeycrisp or Pink Lady apple
2 tablespoons freshly squeezed lemon juice
2 ribs celery, thinly sliced on the diagonal
¼ cup chopped dried cherries
8 slices seed and nut bread or Two-Day Multigrain bread
   (page 301), toasted
8 leaves romaine lettuce, torn
1 cup alfalfa sprouts or your favorite sprout

1. Preheat the oven to 350°F.

2. Season the turkey breast on all sides with 2 teaspoons of the salt and ½ teaspoon of the pepper. Place the turkey in a small roasting pan or on a baking sheet, and roast for 30 minutes. Then brush the turkey with 2 tablespoons of the olive oil and continue to roast for another 30 minutes, or until the thickest section registers an internal temperature of 165°F on an instant-read thermometer. Remove the pan from the oven and loosely tent it with aluminum foil. Let the turkey rest for at least 15 to 20 minutes. Once the turkey has rested, remove the breast bone and cut the turkey into thin slices. Set aside on a platter.

3. To make the Waldorf dressing, in a medium bowl, combine the chopped pecans with the ½ cup yogurt, the ¼ cup mayonnaise, the parsley, and the vinegar. Season with ½ teaspoon salt and ¼ teaspoon pepper.

4. Halve and core the apple; then cut it into thin slices on a mandoline. In a medium bowl, toss the apple slices with the lemon juice, celery, and cherries. Then add the dressing and toss.

5. In a small bowl, combine the remaining 2 tablespoons olive oil, 2 tablespoons yogurt, 2 tablespoons mayonnaise, ¼ teaspoon salt, and ¼ teaspoon pepper. Mix well.

6. To assemble: Place 4 slices of the toast on a clean work surface. Spread 1 tablespoon of the yogurt-mayonnaise mixture on each slice of toast. Top each one with lettuce leaves, several slices of turkey, ¾ cup of the apple salad, and ¼ cup of the sprouts. Top with the remaining slices of toast. Cut each sandwich in half, and serve immediately.

Note: Any leftover roast turkey will keep, well wrapped and refrigerated, for up to 3 days.

# HEIRLOOM TOMATO SANDWICH

4 sandwiches

This is a sandwich to make in the thick of summer when homegrown tomatoes are at their peak. It really is all about the tomato, so don't waste your time making this during the winter months, when those waxy supermarket tomatoes are the only ones available. The Homemade Mayonnaise elevates this embarrassingly simple sandwich to showstopper status. Don't skimp!

5 tablespoons mayonnaise, preferably homemade
    (see page 309)
3 tablespoons chopped fresh basil leaves
8 slices White Sandwich Bread (page 303)
1 pound heirloom tomatoes, stemmed and sliced into
    ¼-inch-thick rounds
Kosher salt and freshly ground black pepper,
    for seasoning

1. Combine the mayonnaise and basil in a small mixing bowl. Using a rubber spatula, stir together to mix well.

2. Arrange the bread in a single layer on a clean work surface, and spread the slices liberally with the basil mayonnaise. Layer 1 or 2 slices of tomato on 4 slices of bread. Season the tomatoes generously with a few pinches of salt and pepper. Top each with another piece of bread, and serve immediately.

# EGGPLANT MUFFULETTA

4 sandwiches

This is no ordinary muffuletta. Made with oven-roasted eggplant slices instead of salumi, a homemade New Orleans–style olive salad, and a fresh basil spread, this muffuletta tastes so good you'll never even miss the meat! If you aren't up to making the olive salad yourself, it'll still be enjoyable with one from the store.

2 medium eggplants (about 1½ pounds),
    trimmed and cut into ½-inch-thick rounds
½ cup olive oil
1½ teaspoons salt
½ teaspoon freshly ground black pepper
1 loaf seeded Italian bread
Basil Spread (page 318)
2 cups New Orleans–Style Olive Salad (recipe follows)
4 ounces sliced mozzarella cheese
4 ounces sliced provolone cheese

1. Position an oven rack as close to the broiler unit as possible, and preheat the broiler.

2. Arrange the eggplant slices in a single layer on two lightly greased baking sheets. Using a pastry brush, lightly brush both sides of the slices with the olive oil. Season both sides with the salt and pepper. Broil the eggplant, in batches, until the slices are tender and lightly browned and have released most of their moisture, 10 to 12 minutes. Remove from the oven and keep warm.

3. Reduce the oven temperature to 350°F and move the oven rack to the center position.

4. When you are ready to assemble the sandwiches, slice the loaf of bread in half horizontally. Using a pastry brush, spread the bottom half with a generous amount of Basil Spread.

5. Spread the olive salad (with its olive oil—do not strain) over the top half of the loaf. Layer the sliced mozzarella and provolone on top of the olive salad, and then layer the slices of eggplant. Place the bottom half of the sandwich on top and lightly press. Quickly and carefully turn the loaf over so that the olive salad side is on top.

6. Place the muffuletta on a baking sheet lined with parchment paper, and bake until the cheese has melted, the muffuletta is heated through, and the bread is slightly crisp, about 12 minutes.

7. Remove the baking sheet from the oven and carefully transfer the loaf to a cutting board. Press lightly, and cut the loaf into 4 sections. Serve immediately.

## New Orleans–Style Olive Salad

About 2 quarts

Don't let the ingredient list scare you—these are all familiar ingredients, and once this salad is stirred together, all the work is done. I personally love making a big batch of this because it's so delicious on so many things and it lasts practically forever in the fridge . . . but if you like, it is easily halved for a smaller batch.

1 quart large pimento-stuffed green olives, drained and roughly chopped
1½ cups large Greek black olives, drained, pitted, and halved
1½ cups extra-virgin olive oil

1½ cups vegetable oil

1 cup pickled cauliflower, drained

3 to 4 ribs celery, thinly sliced on the diagonal

2 medium carrots, thinly sliced on the diagonal

½ cup pepperoncini, drained and halved

⅓ cup cocktail onions, drained

¼ cup nonpareil capers, drained

2 tablespoons minced garlic

2 teaspoons Emeril's Original Essence or Creole Seasoning (page 9)

1 teaspoon crushed red pepper

½ teaspoon freshly ground black pepper

½ teaspoon celery seeds

2 tablespoons chopped fresh oregano leaves

Combine all the ingredients in a large nonreactive bowl and mix well. Place in a large nonreactive jar (preferably glass) and store, tightly covered, in the refrigerator. The salad should be made at least 24 hours before using and only improves with age. You can keep it for up to 2 months in the refrigerator.

Roasted Beets with Pistachio-Goat Cheese
Spread on Sourdough, see pages 49–50

# LUNCHBOX
# SANDWICHES THAT TRAVEL!

# EGG SALAD SUPREME

6 sandwiches, about 3 cups filling

Here's a simple, delicious sandwich. The dry mustard and paprika give it a wonderful surprising wasabi-y or horseradish-y accent.

12 hard-boiled eggs

½ teaspoon salt

1 teaspoon dry mustard

½ teaspoon hot Hungarian paprika

¼ cup minced shallot

¼ cup chopped green onion or fresh parsley leaves

¼ cup minced celery

½ cup mayonnaise, homemade (see page 309) or store-bought

12 slices White Sandwich Bread (page 303)

1. Roughly chop the eggs and place them in a mixing bowl. Add the salt, mustard, paprika, shallot, green onion, celery, and mayonnaise. Stir with a rubber spatula or a spoon until very well blended. Transfer to a container, cover, and refrigerate for at least 2 hours and up to 4 days.

2. Spread ⅓ to ½ cup of the egg salad between 2 slices of bread. Repeat with the remaining salad and bread.

# OLIVE OIL–POACHED TUNA SALAD SANDWICH WITH CITRUS AÏOLI

6 sandwiches

I love a good tuna sandwich made with quality canned tuna as much as the next guy. But this one, with fresh tuna steaks poached in herb oil, is surely kicked up, no ifs, ands, or buts about it. Give it a try the next time you've got a hankering for tuna salad.

2 cups olive oil

6 cloves garlic, smashed

4 sprigs fresh thyme

6 sprigs fresh tarragon, plus ¼ teaspoon chopped
    fresh tarragon leaves

1 small sprig fresh rosemary

7 black peppercorns

1½ teaspoons salt

⅛ teaspoon crushed red pepper

6 thin orange slices

6 thin lemon slices

1¼ pounds tuna, cut into four 1-inch-thick steaks

¼ cup minced shallot

¼ cup finely grated Parmigiano-Reggiano cheese

1 tablespoon minced fresh chives

1 tablespoon chopped fresh parsley leaves

⅛ teaspoon cayenne pepper

1 recipe Citrus Aïoli (page 314)

12 slices sourdough sandwich bread

Lettuce for serving (optional)

Tomato slices, for serving (optional)

Dill pickle slices, for serving (optional)

1. Combine the olive oil, garlic, thyme sprigs, tarragon sprigs, rosemary sprig, peppercorns, salt, crushed red pepper, and orange and lemon slices in a 2½-quart pot. Bring to a simmer over low heat, and then remove from the heat. Let it sit for at least 20 minutes to allow the flavors to infuse.

2. Submerge the tuna steaks in the citrus-herb oil and return the pot to medium heat. Bring to a simmer, and poach the tuna for 2 minutes. Cover the pot with a lid and simmer the tuna for 2 minutes longer. Remove the pot from the heat and allow the tuna to sit in the warm oil for 30 minutes longer. Then remove the tuna from the oil and set it aside to cool. Reserve ⅔ cup of the oil for making the Citrus Aïoli, and discard the remaining oil.

3. Once the tuna has cooled, chop it and place it in a mixing bowl. Add the shallot, Parmesan, chives, parsley, chopped tarragon, and cayenne, and mix well. Fold in the Citrus Aïoli. Transfer the tuna salad to a small container, cover, and refrigerate for at least 30 minutes and up to overnight to allow the flavors to mingle.

4. To assemble: Spread ⅓ cup of the tuna filling between 2 slices of bread. Repeat with the remaining tuna salad and bread. Serve with lettuce, tomato, and dill pickle slices on the side for guests to use, if desired.

# THREE-CHEESE VEGGIE SANDWICH

4 sandwiches

This is a hearty vegetarian sandwich that's packed with flavor. It is absolutely satisfying. I made my own sun-dried tomato pesto and threw in some walnuts for a nice crunch factor, but use your favorite store-bought pesto if you like.

8 slices seeded or multigrain bread (see page 301), toasted

1 cup Sun-Dried Tomato and Walnut Pesto (page 320)

½ cucumber, sliced into ⅛-inch-thick rounds

Salt and freshly ground black pepper, for seasoning

4 slices provolone cheese

4 slices cheddar cheese

4 slices Swiss cheese

½ avocado, thinly sliced

½ cup thinly sliced sun-dried tomatoes

1 cup alfalfa or green leaf sprouts

1 teaspoon olive oil

1. Arrange the toast slices in a single layer on a work surface. Spread 2 tablespoons of the Sun-Dried Tomato and Walnut Pesto on each slice of bread. On 4 of the slices, arrange the cucumber in a single layer, covering as much of the bread as possible, and season with just a pinch of salt and pepper. Place a slice each of provolone, cheddar, and Swiss cheese on top of the cucumber. Divide the avocado slices evenly among the sandwiches and season with salt and pepper. Spread 2 tablespoons of the sun-dried tomatoes evenly over the avocado.

2. In a small mixing bowl, toss the sprouts with the olive oil and a pinch of salt and pepper. Spread ¼ cup of the sprouts over the tomatoes on each sandwich. Complete the sandwiches with the remaining slices of toast.

# TERIYAKI-GLAZED PORK TENDERLOIN SANDWICHES WITH SPICY SESAME MAYO

4 sandwiches

Pork tenderloin is a great cut of meat for sandwich making. It certainly isn't the trouble of a giant roast or a whole chicken, and it can be just as delicious. If you pack this sandwich for lunch, put the veggies in a small separate container and add them right before you eat, so that the toast remains intact.

1 medium daikon radish, julienned

1 carrot, julienned

½ small red onion, thinly sliced

1 teaspoon sea salt

¼ cup rice vinegar

3 tablespoons superfine sugar

1 tablespoon cornstarch

1 tablespoon cold water

2 tablespoons granulated sugar

½ cup soy sauce

½ cup mirin

1 clove garlic, minced

1 teaspoon grated fresh ginger

One 1-pound pork tenderloin, trimmed

4 hoagie rolls, split

½ cup Spicy Sesame Mayo (page 313)

4 to 8 Bibb lettuce leaves, torn into bite-size pieces

1. In a medium mixing bowl, combine the daikon, carrot, and red onion. Sprinkle with the salt and let stand for 30 minutes.

2. In a small mixing bowl, combine the rice vinegar and superfine sugar, stirring until the sugar is dissolved. Pour the vinegar mixture over the daikon mixture, cover, and refrigerate for at least 2 hours and up to 24 hours.

3. In a medium saucepan, combine the cornstarch, water, granulated sugar, soy sauce, mirin, garlic, and grated ginger, and stir the mixture well. Bring to a boil. Then reduce the heat to low and simmer for 2 to 3 minutes. Remove from the heat and set aside to cool. The teriyaki glaze can be stored in a covered container in the refrigerator for up to 1 week.

4. Preheat the oven to 425°F.

5. Brush the tenderloin with the glaze and place it on a baking sheet or roasting pan. Roast the tenderloin until an instant-read thermometer registers 140° to 145°F, about 20 minutes, basting with the glaze after 10 minutes.

6. Remove the pan from the oven and allow the tenderloin to rest for at least 10 minutes. Then thinly slice it crosswise.

7. To assemble: Toast the rolls briefly in the oven. Spread 1 tablespoon of the Spicy Sesame Mayo over each piece of toasted roll. Divide the pork slices among the 4 bottom halves, and top with the lettuce and the pickled vegetables. Add the tops of the rolls and serve immediately.

# WHITE BEAN HUMMUS WITH ROASTED VEGGIES ON LAVASH

4 wraps

Lavash, a wonderful bread from the Middle East, is often known as cracker bread; however, it can also be enjoyed as a soft, thin flatbread and makes for a delicious and hearty wrap. In this recipe it is filled with moist roasted vegetables, flavorful white bean hummus, and a sprinkling of feta cheese, which adds the perfect "zing" to bring it all together. (If you are short on time, you can skip making the white bean hummus and use your favorite store-bought hummus in its place.)

1 large head garlic, top quarter trimmed off

3 tablespoons olive oil

1 teaspoon kosher salt, plus more for seasoning

Freshly ground black pepper, for seasoning

½ large red onion, unpeeled, cut into 2 wedges, leaving the core attached

1 medium zucchini, trimmed and halved lengthwise

2 medium red bell peppers

One 15-ounce can cannellini beans, drained and rinsed

¼ cup extra-virgin olive oil

2 tablespoons tahini (sesame paste)

1 teaspoon freshly squeezed lemon juice

½ teaspoon red wine vinegar

2 cups chopped romaine lettuce

1½ tablespoons Balsamic-Herb Vinaigrette (page 329)
   or store-bought balsamic vinaigrette

4 pieces spinach-flavored lavash flatbread

4 ounces feta cheese, crumbled


1. Preheat the oven to 400°F.

2. Cut a piece of aluminum foil to measure approximately 8 x 4 inches, and place the garlic, cut side up, on the piece of foil. Drizzle 1½ teaspoons of the olive oil over the garlic, and season with a pinch of salt and black pepper. Fold the edges over and seal the pouch. Transfer it to a large rimmed baking sheet.

3. Drizzle 2 tablespoons of the olive oil over the cut sides of the onion wedges and zucchini halves, and season with a pinch of salt and pepper. Place them, cut side down, on the baking sheet. Cut the sides of the bell peppers in sections, and discard the stems and seeds. Arrange the bell peppers in a single layer, skin side down, on the baking sheet and drizzle with the remaining 1½ teaspoons olive oil. Roast the vegetables until they are caramelized or slightly charred and cooked through, 45 minutes. Remove the baking sheet from the oven. Transfer the peppers to a small bowl and cover with plastic wrap. Reserve the onion and zucchini.

4. Carefully open the foil pouch, and squeeze the roasted garlic cloves into a food processor, discarding the peel. Add the beans, extra-virgin olive oil, tahini, lemon juice, red wine vinegar, and the 1 teaspoon kosher salt, and process until smooth, using a rubber spatula to scrape down the sides of the bowl as necessary. If you would like a thinner hummus, add up to 2 tablespoons water. Transfer the hummus to a small serving bowl.

5. Remove the peel from the onion wedges and cut off the core. Slice the onion lengthwise into ¼-inch-thick slices. Peel the skin off the bell peppers and cut them into ¼-inch-thick strips. Cut the zucchini in half crosswise and then slice the pieces lengthwise into ¼-inch-thick strips.

6. Place the romaine, Balsamic-Herb Vinaigrette, and a few pinches of salt and pepper in a small mixing bowl and toss well to coat.

7. To assemble: Working with one at a time, place a lavash on a work surface, making sure the shorter edge is toward you and the longer side of the wrap is perpendicular. Spread about ¼ cup of the hummus along the bottom, leaving about a 2-inch gap from the edge. Spread one-quarter of the roasted onion slices on top of the hummus, followed by one-quarter of the bell peppers and zucchini. Sprinkle about one-quarter of the feta over the vegetables, and top with ½ cup of the romaine. Roll the lavash into a tight cylinder and cut it in half. Repeat with the remaining ingredients, and serve.

# ROAST BEEF SANDWICH WITH FRENCH ONION DIP AND CRISPY SHALLOTS

4 sandwiches

French onion dip really isn't from France; it is about as American as apple pie. Making the dip from scratch is a cinch. This dip is so good on its own, just grab some potato chips and enjoy.

2 tablespoons olive oil

2 tablespoons butter

1 small yellow onion, thinly sliced

3 large shallots, thinly sliced

3 green onions, thinly sliced, white and green parts reserved separately

1 clove garlic

½ cup mayonnaise, homemade (see page 309), or store-bought

½ cup crème fraîche

1 tablespoon freshly squeezed lemon juice

2 teaspoons sea salt

1 pound thinly sliced roast beef

8 slices sourdough sandwich bread, lightly toasted

Crispy Shallots (recipe follows)

1. In a medium saucepan, heat the olive oil and butter over medium-low heat. Add the yellow onion, shallots, the white portion of the green onions, and the garlic. Cover and cook, stirring occasionally, for 20 minutes, or until the onions are completely soft. (Do not let them caramelize; if they begin to brown, add a little water to the pan.) Remove one-third of the mixture from the pan and set it aside. Transfer the remaining mixture to a blender and puree until smooth.

2. Combine the reserved onion mixture with the pureed onions in a bowl. Add the mayonnaise, crème fraîche, lemon juice, and sea salt, and mix well. Refrigerate, covered, for 2 hours and up to 24 hours.

3. Divide the roast beef among 4 slices of the toast. Spoon 3 tablespoons (or more to taste) of the onion sauce over the roast beef, and sprinkle with the fried shallots. Top with the remaining slices of toast, and serve with the remaining onion sauce on the side, if desired. (Any leftover onion sauce will keep in the refrigerator for up to 3 days and is wonderful with chips.)

## Crispy Shallots

I cup

Crispy shallots are best used the same day they are made. Store in an airtight container after cooling completely.

3 shallots, thinly sliced, rings separated
2 tablespoons Crystal hot sauce or other Louisiana red hot sauce
½ cup all-purpose flour
Vegetable oil, for frying
Sea salt, for seasoning

1. In a small bowl, combine the shallots with the hot sauce. Add the flour to the bowl and toss to coat.

2. Pour vegetable oil in a small saucepan to a depth of 1 to 2 inches, and heat it over medium heat. Fry the shallots, in batches and stirring gently, until golden brown, about 1 minute. Using a slotted spoon, transfer the shallots to a paper-towel-lined plate. Season with sea salt.

# GRILLED CHICKEN AND BACON SANDWICH WITH MINT HONEY MUSTARD

4 sandwiches

Pounding the chicken breast and marinating it in fresh lime juice, herbs, garlic, and ginger makes for a most tender and juicy chicken sandwich. Since this marinade is potent, don't leave the chicken in it for longer than two hours—you want it to be flavor-packed without sacrificing texture.

1 tablespoon minced jalapeño, with seeds

1 tablespoon minced fresh ginger

1 tablespoon minced garlic

2 tablespoons chopped onion

Grated zest of 1 lime

¼ cup freshly squeezed lime juice

2 tablespoons chopped fresh parsley leaves

¼ cup chopped fresh mint leaves

½ cup vegetable oil

1 pound boneless, skinless chicken breasts

1¼ teaspoons kosher salt

½ teaspoon freshly ground black pepper

¼ cup olive oil

8 hamburger buns

Mayonnaise, homemade (see page 309), or store-bought

Mint Honey Mustard (page 319)

8 strips bacon, cooked and cut in half

Tomato slices

Lettuce leaves, torn into pieces

1. Combine the jalapeño, ginger, garlic, onion, lime zest, lime juice, parsley, and mint in a small bowl. Whisk in the vegetable oil.

2. Cut the chicken into 4 equal pieces. Lay each piece between sheets of plastic wrap and beat with a mallet to ½-inch thickness. Place the chicken in a resealable plastic food storage bag, add the marinade, and refrigerate for up to 2 hours.

3. Preheat a grill pan or grill to medium.

4. Remove the chicken from the marinade and lightly pat it dry. Season with the salt and pepper, and drizzle with 2 tablespoons of the olive oil.

5. Add the chicken to the grill pan and cook for 1½ to 2 minutes. Rotate the chicken 90 degrees to make grill cross marks and cook for another 2 minutes. Then turn the chicken over and repeat, cooking until the chicken is nicely browned and cooked through, 6 to 8 minutes total. Remove the chicken from the grill pan and set it aside.

6. Brush the remaining 2 tablespoons olive oil over the insides of the buns, and cook them on the grill pan until toasted. Remove from the pan.

7. To assemble: Spread mayonnaise over the inside of the top halves of the buns. Spread Mint Honey Mustard over the inside of the bottom halves. Add a piece of grilled chicken, 4 pieces of bacon, tomato slices, and lettuce to each bottom half, and cover with the tops. Serve immediately.

# ROASTED BEETS WITH PISTACHIO-GOAT CHEESE SPREAD ON SOURDOUGH

4 sandwiches

The earthiness of beets, a nutty, creamy goat cheese, and spicy arugula make for an awesome combination. Use only the freshest ingredients (farmer's market, here I come . . . ) and a really good sourdough for this sandwich.

8 ounces red beets (about 3 small beets)

5 tablespoons olive oil

1¼ teaspoons sea salt

¾ teaspoon freshly ground black pepper

8 ounces yellow beets (about 3 small beets)

2 tablespoons balsamic vinegar

8 ounces goat cheese, at room temperature

½ cup toasted and chopped pistachios

2 cups baby arugula, rinsed and spun dry

2 cups peppercress or watercress, rinsed and spun dry

8 slices sourdough bread, toasted

¼ cup Onion Jam (page 343)

1. Preheat the oven to 350°F.

2. Place the red beets in a small bowl; drizzle with 1 tablespoon of the olive oil and season with ¼ teaspoon of the salt and ⅛ teaspoon of the pepper. In another small bowl, repeat this process with the yellow beets. Place the red beets on a square of aluminum foil and wrap to form a packet. Do the same for the yellow beets, and then place both packets on a baking sheet. Roast in the oven until tender, 55 to

60 minutes. Remove from the oven and let cool. Once the beets are cool enough to handle, rub them with a paper towel to remove their skins, trim the tops and bottoms to form a flat surface, and then thinly slice the beets on a mandoline, between ⅛ and ¼ inch thick.

3. In a small bowl, combine 2 tablespoons of the olive oil with the balsamic vinegar. Drizzle the red beets with 1 tablespoon of the balsamic–olive oil mixture, season with ¼ teaspoon of the salt and ⅛ teaspoon of the pepper, and set aside. Repeat with the yellow beets. Reserve the remaining 2 tablespoons of the balsamic–olive oil mixture.

4. In a small bowl, mix the goat cheese with the chopped pistachios and the remaining 1 tablespoon olive oil.

5. Toss the arugula and peppercress with the reserved 2 tablespoons balsamic–olive oil mixture, and season with the remaining ¼ teaspoon salt and ¼ teaspoon pepper.

6. Assemble the sandwiches by spreading 1 tablespoon of the goat cheese mixture over each of the 8 slices of toast. Divide the red and yellow beets evenly among 4 slices of the bread, and then spoon 1 tablespoon of the Onion Jam over the beets on each one. Place ½ cup of the greens on top of the onion jam on each sandwich, and then cover with the remaining 4 slices of toast. Cut each sandwich in half and serve immediately.

# CURRIED CHICKEN SALAD ON PUMPERNICKEL

8 sandwiches

Perfectly sweet and savory, this moist sandwich is delectable—just as suitable for a business luncheon as it would be for a bridal shower. Next time you're the host, this is an easy make-ahead choice. And it is as attractive as it is delicious.

2¼ pounds boneless, skinless chicken breasts

2½ cups chicken stock or packaged low-sodium chicken broth

½ cup dry white wine

5 sprigs fresh cilantro,
    plus 2 tablespoons finely chopped fresh cilantro leaves

¼ cup freshly squeezed lemon juice

2 cloves garlic, smashed

1 teaspoon black peppercorns

1½ teaspoons salt, plus more for seasoning

4 green onions: 2 smashed and 2 finely chopped

2 ribs celery, finely chopped

1 cup mayonnaise, homemade (see page 309), or store-bought

1 tablespoon curry powder

¼ teaspoon cayenne pepper

¼ cup golden raisins

2 tablespoons dried currants

16 slices dark pumpernickel bread (see page 295)

1 cup Major Grey's Chutney, or to taste

Freshly ground black pepper, for seasoning

3 ounces baby spinach leaves, rinsed and spun dry

1. Combine the chicken, stock, wine, cilantro sprigs, 2 tablespoons of the lemon juice, the garlic, peppercorns, 1 teaspoon of the salt, and the smashed green onions in a medium saucepan and bring to a gentle boil. Reduce the heat to a bare simmer and cook for 10 minutes. Remove from the heat and allow the chicken to cool in the poaching liquid for 45 minutes. Then remove the chicken from the liquid and set it aside until completely cool. Strain the poaching liquid and reserve it for another purpose if desired. Discard the solids.

2. Cut the chicken into small dice. In a large bowl, combine the chicken, chopped cilantro, remaining 2 tablespoons lemon juice, remaining ½ teaspoon salt, chopped green onions, celery, mayonnaise, curry powder, cayenne, golden raisins, and currants, and stir to blend well. Taste, and adjust the seasoning if necessary. Chill the chicken salad, covered, for at least 2 hours and up to several days in advance.

3. To assemble: Spread one side of each piece of bread with about 1 tablespoon of the chutney. Place about ½ cup of the chicken salad over each of 8 slices. Season lightly with salt and pepper. Divide the spinach among the sandwiches, and top with the remaining 8 slices of bread. Halve the sandwiches and serve immediately, or wrap them in plastic wrap and store them up to overnight, refrigerated, until ready to serve.

Portobello with Ricotta, Arugula,
and Truffle Oil on Brioche
see pages 77–80

# ON A Roll

# CHILI DOG

Oh, baby, this isn't your ordinary chili dog. The chili recipe is inspired by the immensely popular chili served at my restaurant in Bethlehem, Pennsylvania, Burgers and More. The surprise ingredient is roux, and boy, does it make for an awesome-flavored chili. This chili also gets its color from pureed peppers instead of the more typical tomato sauce. Guests can't get enough of it.

One 8-ounce jar roasted red bell peppers

One 12-ounce jar sweet cherry peppers

¼ cup plus 2 teaspoons vegetable oil

¼ cup plus 2 tablespoons all-purpose flour

1 cup finely chopped onion

½ cup finely chopped celery

1 tablespoon minced garlic

1 pound ground beef

2 tablespoons chili powder

1 tablespoon onion powder

1 tablespoon sweet paprika

1½ teaspoons ground coriander

1½ teaspoons ground cumin

1½ teaspoons garlic powder

1 teaspoon salt

1½ cups chicken stock or packaged low-sodium chicken broth

8 extra-long hot dogs

8 long hot dog buns, sliced open

1 cup shredded sharp cheddar cheese

½ cup finely chopped red onion, for garnish

1. Strain the roasted bell peppers and discard all but 2 tablespoons of the liquid. Add the peppers and liquid to a blender, along with 8 of the cherry peppers and ¼ cup of the liquid from the cherry pepper jar. Process until thoroughly pureed. Transfer to a bowl and set aside.

2. Heat the vegetable oil in an 8-quart stockpot over medium-high heat. Add the flour and begin whisking immediately. Switch to a wooden spoon and cook, stirring continuously, until the roux has reached a deep brown color and smells nutty, about 5 minutes. Add the onion, celery, and garlic and cook until fragrant, about 2 minutes. Add the beef, chili powder, onion powder, paprika, coriander, cumin, garlic powder, and salt and cook, stirring, until the beef is cooked through, about 4 minutes. Add the pureed peppers and the chicken stock, and stir well to combine. Bring to a simmer and continue to cook, stirring occasionally, until the flavors come together and the chili has thickened, about 30 minutes.

3. Position an oven rack in the center and preheat the oven to 350°F.

4. Heat a grill pan over medium-high heat (if you don't have one, a nonstick sauté pan will suffice). Using a knife, make two diagonal slits on each side of the hot dogs. In batches, cook the hot dogs in the grill pan until they are blistered and hatch marks appear, about 3 minutes per side. Nestle a hot dog in each of the buns and place them on a parchment-lined baking sheet. Ladle enough chili over the hot dogs to cover them, and then sprinkle 2 tablespoons of the cheese over each.

5. Warm the hot dogs in the oven until the cheese has melted and the bread is lightly toasted, about 5 minutes. Remove from the oven, garnish with the chopped red onion, and serve immediately.

Note: Any leftover chili will keep, covered and refrigerated, for up to 1 week.

# BBQ PORK RIBS, CHINESE STYLE

24 small sandwiches, 6 to 8 servings

Authentic Chinese barbecue is pretty simple to do at home. These ribs need to marinate for a while, but the rest of it is a walk in the park. This recipe was inspired by Chinese pork buns, such as those you might find as a dim sum offering in Chinatown. King's Hawaiian Sweet Rolls are a great substitute for the traditional Chinese buns because they're soft and sweet; you can pretty much find them anywhere.

¾ cup hoisin sauce

⅔ cup soy sauce

½ cup dry sherry

¼ cup sugar

¼ cup ketchup (see page 339)

1½ teaspoons Chinese five-spice powder

1 teaspoon hot sesame oil

3 cloves garlic, minced

2 green onions, minced

4 pounds country-style pork ribs

½ cup hot water

24 small soft rolls, such as King's Hawaiian Sweet Rolls or
    Potato Rolls (page 293), cut in half

1 cup thinly sliced cucumber

Pickled Green Onions (recipe follows)

1. In a large mixing bowl, combine ½ cup of the hoisin sauce with the soy sauce, sherry, sugar, ketchup, five-spice powder, sesame oil, garlic, and green onions, and mix well. Remove 1 cup of the marinade, cover it, and refrigerate.

2. Place the pork ribs in a resealable plastic food storage bag or other container, and add the remaining marinade. Refrigerate for at least 5 hours and up to overnight.

3. Position an oven rack in the top third of the oven, and preheat the oven to 325°F.

4. Line a rimmed baking sheet with aluminum foil and set a rack on top. Pour the hot water onto the bottom of the baking sheet. Place the ribs on the rack. Wrap aluminum foil over the ribs and around the baking sheet so that they will steam. Place the baking sheet in the oven and cook for 25 minutes.

5. Remove the foil and cook for another 40 to 45 minutes, or until the ribs are fork-tender. Remove the ribs from the oven and raise the oven setting to broil.

6. Brush the ribs with some of the reserved marinade, and broil the ribs for 5 minutes. Remove the ribs from the oven, turn them over, brush with more of the reserved marinade, and broil for 5 minutes. Continue this process until the ribs are well glazed and have turned a dark brown, 3 to 5 minutes longer.

7. Remove the ribs from the oven and let them cool to room temperature. Remove the meat from the bones and toss it in the remaining reserved marinade. Discard the bones.

8. To assemble: Spread the remaining ¼ cup hoisin sauce on the top halves of the rolls. Mound the chopped meat on the bottom halves, and top each one with several slices of cucumber, a pickled green onion, and then the top half of the roll. Serve immediately.

# Pickled Green Onions

½ cup sugar

½ cup white wine vinegar

½ cup water

1½ teaspoons salt

1 teaspoon Korean chili flakes or crushed red pepper

½ teaspoon mustard seeds

½ teaspoon coriander seeds

4 bunches green onions, trimmed to 5-inch lengths

1. In a medium saucepan, combine everything but the green onions and bring to a boil over medium heat, stirring until the sugar is dissolved.

2. Place the green onions in a glass jar or other heatproof container. Pour the hot pickling mixture over them and immediately cover with a lid. Chill in the refrigerator for at least 1 hour or up to 3 days before serving.

# FRIED FISH SANDWICHES WITH JICAMA COLESLAW

6 sandwiches

Fried fish sandwiches remind me of summer at the shore. East Coast, West Coast, or Gulf Coast, you're going to find some kind of truck, stand, or shack selling fish sandwiches. Use any kind of flaky white fish you can find; just make sure it's fresh and from as close to home as you can get.

Vegetable oil, for frying

1 cup all-purpose flour

2 tablespoons chili powder

1 teaspoon chipotle chile powder

1½ teaspoons salt, plus more for seasoning

½ teaspoon cayenne pepper

2 eggs

2 tablespoons water

1¼ pounds halibut or other whitefish fillets, cut into ¼-inch-thick pieces

6 buttermilk hot dog buns, sliced open

2 tablespoons butter, melted

½ cup plus 1 tablespoon Jalapeño Mayo (page 311)

2 cups Jicama Coleslaw (recipe follows)

Chopped fresh cilantro leaves, for garnish

Sea salt and vinegar-flavored potato chips, or your favorite, for serving (optional)

1. Fill a large cast-iron or other heavy-bottomed pot with vegetable oil to a depth of 3 inches, and heat it to 350°F.

2. In a medium bowl, combine the flour, chili powder, chipotle powder, ½ teaspoon of the salt, and the cayenne and mix well. In a separate bowl, whisk the eggs with the water until well beaten.

3. Preheat the oven to 250°F.

4. Season the fish with the remaining 1 teaspoon salt. Dredge each piece of fish in the seasoned flour, coating it completely. Then dip each piece in the egg wash, letting the excess drip off. Dredge the fish for a second time in the flour mixture, coating it completely. Working in batches, fry the fish in the hot oil until it is crisp, golden brown, and just cooked through, 2 to 3 minutes. Transfer the fish to paper towels to drain briefly, and season it lightly with salt.

5. Brush the hot dog buns with the melted butter, and warm them in the oven for 2 to 3 minutes.

6. Spread 1½ tablespoons of the Jalapeño Mayo on each hot dog bun. Divide the fish among the buns, and top each one with ⅓ cup of the coleslaw. Garnish with chopped cilantro. Serve the sandwiches with the potato chips, if desired.

## Jicama Coleslaw

About I generous quart

1 small jicama, peeled and julienned (about 2 cups)

1 chayote, peeled and julienned (about 1 cup)

1 cup thinly sliced red onion

1 cup thinly sliced orange bell pepper

2 thinly sliced jalapeños, with seeds

¼ cup mayonnaise, homemade (see page 309), or store-bought

¼ cup buttermilk (see Note)

¼ cup freshly squeezed lime juice

1 tablespoon Dijon mustard

1 teaspoon salt

1 teaspoon sugar

½ teaspoon cayenne pepper

In a medium bowl, combine the jicama, chayote, red onion, bell pepper, jalapeños, mayonnaise, buttermilk, lime juice, Dijon mustard, salt, sugar, and cayenne. Mix well and refrigerate for at least 1 hour and up to overnight.

Note: If you don't have buttermilk on hand, you can make your own by adding 1 tablespoon distilled white vinegar to 1 cup whole milk. Stir to blend and set aside until thickened and creamy, usually about 5 minutes; then use as needed.

# BARBECUED TURKEY SANDWICHES WITH CLASSIC COLESLAW

*8 sandwiches*

Think pulled pork made with turkey instead! These sandwiches give my beloved pulled pork a run for its money. If you don't have time or just don't feel like making the Kansas City–Style Barbecue Sauce, feel free to use your favorite store-bought variety.

5 pounds turkey legs (about 5)

2 teaspoons salt

1 teaspoon freshly ground black pepper

2 teaspoons olive oil

1 onion, quartered

2 cloves garlic, chopped

1 bay leaf

4 cups chicken stock or packaged low-sodium

   chicken broth

6 cups water

1 recipe Kansas City–Style Barbecue Sauce (page 342)

8 sesame seed hamburger buns

Classic Coleslaw (recipe follows)

1. Season the turkey legs with the salt and pepper. Heat a large Dutch oven over medium-high heat, and add the olive oil. When it is hot, add the turkey legs and cook until browned on all sides, about 15 minutes. Add the onion and garlic and cook, stirring occasionally, until the onion is golden brown, about 4 minutes. Add the bay leaf, chicken stock, and water, and bring to a boil. Reduce the heat to

medium-low, cover, and simmer for 2 to 2½ hours, or until the meat is tender and beginning to pull away from the bone.

2. Remove the turkey legs from the broth and set them aside to cool. Once they are cool enough to handle, remove and discard the skin. Shred the meat and discard the bones. Strain and reserve the stock for another use.

3. Heat the barbecue sauce in a medium saucepan over medium heat. Add the shredded turkey to the sauce and cook until it is just warmed through.

4. Spoon the turkey onto the bottom halves of the buns. Add the coleslaw and the top halves of the buns. Serve immediately.

## Classic Coleslaw

8 servings

¾ cup mayonnaise, homemade (see page 309),
    or store-bought
¼ cup Dijon mustard
¼ cup packed light brown sugar
3 tablespoons cider vinegar
2 tablespoons buttermilk (see Note, page 64)
4 teaspoons celery seeds
1 teaspoon salt, plus more for seasoning
¼ teaspoon freshly ground black pepper,
    plus more for seasoning
⅛ teaspoon cayenne pepper
3 cups shredded green cabbage (about ½ head)
3 cups shredded red cabbage (about ½ head)
1 yellow bell pepper, finely diced
1 large carrot, shredded

½ cup grated yellow onion

¼ cup minced fresh parsley leaves

1. In a bowl, combine the mayonnaise, mustard, brown sugar, vinegar, buttermilk, celery seeds, salt, pepper, and cayenne. Whisk well to dissolve the sugar.

2. In a large bowl, combine the cabbage, bell pepper, carrot, onion, and parsley. Toss with the dressing until evenly coated. Adjust the seasoning to taste. Refrigerate until chilled, at least 2 hours and up to overnight, before serving.

# PORK TONKATSU WITH PICKLED VEGETABLES

4 sandwiches

Pork cutlets breaded in panko breadcrumbs and drizzled with tonkatsu sauce is a popular Japanese dish that makes one incredible sandwich. Tonkatsu sauce can be found at your local Asian market or in the ethnic aisle of your local grocery store; however, if you have a difficult time finding it, you can just substitute your favorite steak sauce.

1 pound pork tenderloin, cut crosswise into four 2-inch pieces
    (about 4 ounces each)
½ teaspoon salt
⅛ teaspoon freshly ground black pepper
¼ cup all-purpose flour
2 eggs, beaten
1 cup panko breadcrumbs
¼ cup vegetable oil, plus more for pan-frying and brushing
4 large Brioche Buns or Potato Rolls, cut in half,
    or eight ½-inch-thick slices brioche bread
    (pages 272 and 293)
¼ cup plus 1 tablespoon mayonnaise, homemade (see page 309),
    or store-bought
6 tablespoons tonkatsu sauce or your favorite steak sauce
Pickled Vegetables (recipe follows), for garnish
4 small leaves red-leaf lettuce

1. Using the smooth side of a meat mallet, pound the pork against the grain to a thickness of ¼ inch. Season on both sides with the salt and pepper.

2. Put the flour, eggs, and breadcrumbs in separate shallow dishes. Bread the cutlets one at a time by first dredging them in the flour, shaking to remove any excess, then dipping them in the beaten eggs, letting any excess drip off, and then dipping them in the panko. Set aside.

3. In a 10-inch skillet, heat the ¼ cup oil over medium-high heat. When it is hot, reduce the heat to medium. Cook the pork, in batches, until golden brown, about 5 minutes per side. Add more oil as necessary between batches. Transfer the cooked pork to a cooling rack set over a baking sheet lined with paper towels. Let it rest for about 10 minutes.

4. Wipe the skillet clean with a paper towel and return it to medium-high heat. Brush the cut side of each brioche bun lightly with oil. In batches, toast the buns, oiled side down, in the skillet.

5. To assemble: Arrange the brioche buns in a single layer on a work surface, toasted sides facing up. Spread each half with about 2 teaspoons of the mayonnaise. Divide the crispy pork evenly among the bottom halves. Drizzle each sandwich with 1½ tablespoons of the tonkatsu sauce, and then layer it with 5 to 6 slices of pickled zucchini, 2 to 3 slices of pickled carrot, and about 1 tablespoon of pickled onions. Add a lettuce leaf on top of the pickled vegetables, and place the brioche top, toasted side down, on top. Serve immediately.

## Pickled Vegetables

About 2 generous cups

These pickled veggies are also great for snacking.

1 medium carrot
1 medium zucchini
½ small yellow onion, thinly sliced

1 tablespoon kosher salt

½ cup rice vinegar

3 tablespoons soy sauce

1 tablespoon dark brown sugar

1 teaspoon minced fresh ginger

1 tablespoon hot sesame oil

1. Using a vegetable peeler, slice the carrot lengthwise into thin ribbons. Stack the ribbons and then cut them in half crosswise to form 3- to 4-inch lengths.

2. Trim the zucchini and slice it into ⅛-inch-thick rounds. Place the zucchini, carrot, and onion in a medium mixing bowl and add the salt. Toss well to coat, and then add enough cold water to cover plus a couple of handfuls of ice cubes. Stir to mix well. Set aside at room temperature for about 1 hour.

3. Test the vegetables for texture; when they are ready they will feel slightly softened and taste a bit salty. Drain and dry them well, using paper towels to remove any remaining moisture. Place the vegetables in a small resealable plastic food storage bag.

4. In a small mixing bowl, whisk together the rice vinegar, soy sauce, brown sugar, and ginger. While continuing to whisk, slowly drizzle in the sesame oil in a slow, steady stream. Pour the mixture over the vegetables, seal the bag, and place the bag in a small bowl in the refrigerator. Chill for at least 4 hours and up to overnight, turning the bag occasionally to ensure even pickling.

# SEARED SALMON WITH GINGERED RADISH PICKLE AND SOY MAYO ON A ROLL

4 large sandwiches, 4 to 8 servings

This is not your ordinary fish sandwich. Marinated salmon fillets are seared and served with pickled radish (tasting a bit like the pickled ginger you get at the sushi bar) on King's Hawaiian Savory Butter Rolls. This bread is dynamite. If you can't find it, pick up a pack of potato rolls instead—or make your own (see page 293).

Four 6- to 8-ounce skinless salmon fillets

6 tablespoons chopped green onion

6 tablespoons chopped fresh cilantro leaves

2 tablespoons sugar

4½ teaspoons minced fresh ginger

4½ teaspoons minced garlic

1½ teaspoons crushed red pepper

3 tablespoons rice vinegar

¼ cup plus 2 tablespoons soy sauce

¼ cup plus 2 tablespoons dark Asian sesame oil

½ cup plus 2 tablespoons vegetable oil

Four 4-packs King's Hawaiian Savory Butter Rolls, or
    4 other soft rolls measuring about 4 x 6 inches

Salt and freshly ground black pepper, for seasoning

1 bunch watercress, rinsed and spun dry, large stems removed

½ cup thinly sliced red onion

1 tablespoon extra-virgin olive oil

Soy Mayo (page 313)

Gingered Radish Pickle (recipe follows)

1. Place the salmon in a gallon-size resealable plastic food storage bag. In a small bowl, combine the green onion, cilantro, sugar, ginger, garlic, crushed red pepper, rice vinegar, soy sauce, sesame oil, and 6 tablespoons of the vegetable oil. Whisk together and pour over the salmon. Close the bag and refrigerate for at least 2 and up to 4 hours, turning the bag at least once to ensure even marination. Remove the fillets from the marinade (discard the marinade) and keep them, covered, in the refrigerator until ready to cook or up to overnight.

2. Heat a medium skillet over medium heat. If you're using the King's Hawaiian rolls, leave each 4-pack intact and slice them in half horizontally (each 4-pack makes 1 large sandwich). Lightly brush the cut sides of the rolls with 2 tablespoons vegetable oil. Working in batches, add the rolls to the skillet, oiled side down, and cook until toasted. Set aside.

3. Season the salmon with salt and pepper. Raise the heat under the skillet to high, and add 1 tablespoon vegetable oil to the skillet. Working in batches, add the fillets and cook, turning them once, until golden brown on both sides, about 5 minutes for medium, depending on the thickness of the fillets. Add the final 1 tablespoon of oil as needed. Set aside.

4. Combine the watercress and red onion in a small bowl, and drizzle with the extra-virgin olive oil. Season lightly with salt and pepper, and toss to combine.

5. To assemble: Spread Soy Mayo on both halves of the rolls. Add the watercress salad to the bottom halves, and then the salmon fillets. Drain the liquid from the Gingered Radish Pickle, and lay the pickles on top of the salmon fillets. Top with the top halves of the rolls.

# Gingered Radish Pickle

1 cup thinly sliced radish (cut on a mandoline if possible)

2 tablespoons seeded and minced jalapeño

⅓ cup rice vinegar

2 tablespoons mirin

2 tablespoons minced fresh ginger

1 tablespoon sugar

1 teaspoon salt

Combine the radish and jalapeño in a small bowl. In a small saucepan, combine the rice vinegar, mirin, ginger, sugar, and salt. Bring the mixture to a boil, and then pour it over the radishes and jalapeño. Set aside until cooled. Cover, and refrigerate up to several days until ready to use.

# PORTOBELLO WITH RICOTTA, ARUGULA, AND TRUFFLE OIL ON BRIOCHE

4 large sandwiches

The truffle oil alone kicks this sandwich up a notch! Start drizzling, and they start coming. Hand them this indulgent veggie sandwich and watch them lap it up, bite after bite.

1 cup thinly sliced red onion

1 pound leeks, tops and roots removed,
    well washed and thinly sliced

½ cup thinly sliced shallot

2 sprigs fresh thyme

¾ teaspoon salt, plus more for seasoning

¼ teaspoon freshly ground black pepper,
    plus more for seasoning

½ cup extra-virgin olive oil

1½ pounds portobello mushroom caps,
    trimmed

1 cup ricotta cheese, drained

¼ cup Roasted Garlic (recipe follows)

4 Brioche Buns, store-bought or
    homemade (page 272), cut in half

¼ cup truffle oil or very good-quality
    extra-virgin olive oil

2 cups arugula, rinsed and spun dry

1 cup alfalfa or radish sprouts

1 teaspoon freshly squeezed lemon juice

2 Roasted Bell Peppers (recipe follows),

   or 1 cup jarred

Tomato slices, for serving

Avocado slices, for serving

1. Preheat the oven to 400°F.

2. Combine the red onion, leeks, shallot, and thyme sprigs in a bowl. Season with ⅛ teaspoon of the salt and ⅛ teaspoon of the pepper, and toss with ¼ cup of the extra-virgin olive oil. Transfer to a baking sheet and roast for 20 minutes, stirring midway through, until soft. Set aside to cool. Discard the thyme sprigs.

3. Season the mushrooms with ⅛ teaspoon of the salt and ⅛ teaspoon of the pepper, and toss them with the remaining ¼ cup extra-virgin olive oil. Transfer the mushrooms to a baking sheet, and roast for 10 minutes. Remove from the oven and set aside to cool. (If you have two baking sheets, you can roast the onion mixture and the mushrooms at the same time, of course.)

4. In a small bowl, combine the ricotta with the cooled onion mixture, roasted garlic, and the remaining ½ teaspoon salt.

5. Hollow out some of the top of the brioche buns by pinching and removing some of the bread. Set the buns, cut side up, on a baking sheet and toast in the oven until lightly browned, about 5 minutes. Remove from the oven and drizzle 1 teaspoon of the truffle oil over each half.

6. In a bowl, gently toss the arugula and sprouts with the lemon juice and the remaining 4 teaspoons truffle oil. Season lightly with salt and pepper.

7. To assemble: Spread about 2 tablespoons of the ricotta mixture over both halves of each bun. Layer the bottom buns with the mushrooms, and season lightly with salt and pepper. Add the roasted pepper pieces, tomato slices, and avocado slices, continuing

to lightly season between the layers. Divide the arugula salad among the sandwiches, and place the remaining bun halves on top.

## Roasted Garlic

¼ cup

If you want more than the amount of roasted garlic called for in this recipe, just increase it—roasting ten heads of garlic takes no more time than two. Add any leftover roasted garlic to pizza, pasta, and mashed potatoes for extra yumminess there, too.

2 heads garlic
1 tablespoon olive oil

1. Preheat the oven to 400°F.

2. Cut a piece of aluminum foil to measure approximately 8 x 8 inches. Slice off and discard the top quarter of each head of garlic, and place the garlic heads, cut side up, on the foil. Drizzle the olive oil over the garlic. Fold the foil around the garlic to form a pouch. Place the pouch on a baking sheet, and roast until the cloves are soft and golden brown, about 40 minutes. Remove the pouch from the oven, open the foil, and let it sit until the garlic is cool enough to handle.

3. Squeeze each garlic head, gently pressing it with your fingers to expel the soft cloves into a bowl. Stir the garlic with a rubber spatula and blend it thoroughly, if desired. Use immediately, or store, covered, in the refrigerator for up to 2 weeks.

# Roasted Bell Peppers

2 roasted peppers

2 red, yellow, or orange bell peppers

1 tablespoon olive oil

1. Preheat the oven to 400°F.

2. Brush the bell peppers all over with the olive oil, and place them on a rimmed baking sheet. Roast, turning the peppers over about halfway through, until blackened on a couple of sides, about 20 minutes.

3. Remove the peppers from the oven, place them in a bowl, and cover it with plastic wrap. After about 5 minutes, the skin will have loosened. Remove the plastic wrap. When the peppers are cool enough to handle, slide off the skins and discard them along with the stems and seeds. The peppers should separate into nice wide sections.

# BLUE CHEESE–STUFFED SKILLET BURGER WITH GREEN PEPPERCORN MAYO

6 burgers

Crank up the stove. Turn your exhaust fan on high. Get that skillet smokin'. You're about to cook! Getting that crisped, charred exterior while keeping a juicy interior is the beauty of a skillet burger. This one has creamy blue cheese inside that melts just as you take a bite, and an extraordinary tangy-peppery mayo. Oh, yeah, babe.

2½ pounds boneless beef chuck roast,
    coarsely ground by your butcher,
    or 85% lean ground chuck

3 tablespoons Worcestershire sauce

1 tablespoon minced garlic

1 tablespoon chopped fresh thyme leaves

1½ teaspoons salt

6 ounces blue cheese,
    such as Roquefort or Maytag,
    cut into six 1-ounce chunks

6 Kaiser rolls, cut in half

¼ cup plus 2 tablespoons vegetable oil

½ teaspoon coarse salt

Green Peppercorn Mayo (page 310)

Lettuce leaves, for serving

Tomato slices, for serving

Red onion slices, for serving

1. Put the beef in a mixing bowl, and add the Worcestershire, garlic, thyme, and salt. Using clean hands, gently toss the mixture to combine. Divide the mixture into 6 portions and form them into balls.

2. Make a deep hole in the middle of a burger with your fingers. Press a chunk of blue cheese inside the hole, and then fold the edges of the burger over the cheese to enclose it completely. With the palm of your hand, flatten the burger into a thick 4-inch-wide disk, and then pinch all around the edges to seal in the filling. Set the stuffed burger aside on a parchment-lined tray. Repeat with the remaining burgers. Cover and refrigerate until ready to cook.

3. Heat a large cast-iron skillet over high heat. Liberally brush the insides of the Kaiser rolls with the vegetable oil. Add the rolls to the hot skillet, cut sides down, and cook until toasted, 3 to 5 minutes. Remove them from the skillet and set aside. Wipe the skillet clean with a paper towel, and return it to high heat.

4. Sprinkle ¼ teaspoon of the coarse salt in the hot skillet. Add 3 of the burgers and cook, without moving them, until a deep crust is formed, about 3 minutes. Flip the burgers onto the other side and cook for 2 to 3 minutes longer. Remove the burgers from the skillet and set aside. Discard the oil in the skillet, scrape up and discard the drippings, wipe the skillet clean, and repeat with the remaining burgers.

5. To assemble: Spread Green Peppercorn Mayonnaise on both sides of a Kaiser roll. Add a burger and dress it with the lettuce, tomato, and red onion. Repeat with the remaining burgers. Serve immediately.

# GARDEN BURGER
# WITH CRANBERRY CHUTNEY

4 burgers

You have never tasted a veggie burger this good, trust me! I like to serve it
simply dressed with mixed greens and a cranberry vinaigrette topped with
a little cranberry chutney. But hey, dress it however you like and enjoy.

2 tablespoons grapeseed oil

½ cup chopped yellow onion

2 teaspoons chopped garlic

½ cup chopped red bell pepper

¼ cup chopped celery

½ cup chopped walnuts

2 cups firm-cooked lentils,
    preferably lentilles du Puy

1 cup cooked wild rice or brown rice

¼ cup chopped dried cranberries or
    dried currants

¼ cup whole wheat breadcrumbs

1 teaspoon chopped fresh basil leaves

½ teaspoon chopped fresh thyme leaves

½ teaspoon chopped fresh oregano leaves

2 large eggs, lightly beaten

2 tablespoons whole wheat flour

2 tablespoons milk

Salt and freshly ground black pepper,
    to taste

½ cup instant flour, such as Wondra

2 tablespoons olive oil

4 whole wheat hamburger buns

2 tablespoons butter, melted

4 cups mixed salad greens

Cranberry Vinaigrette (page 331)

¼ cup Cranberry Chutney (page 340),
     or more to taste

1. Heat a small sauté pan over medium-high heat, and add the grapeseed oil. When it is hot, add the onion, garlic, bell pepper, and celery, and cook for about 10 minutes, or until the onion is translucent. Remove from the heat and let cool.

2. In a large bowl, combine the sautéed vegetables with the walnuts, lentils, rice, cranberries, breadcrumbs, basil, thyme, oregano, eggs, whole wheat flour, and milk. Season with salt and pepper, and mix well. Form the lentil mixture into 4 patties, using about ¾ cup per burger. The mix will be fairly crumbly and you may need to squeeze the patties slightly to remove any excess moisture. Dust the patties with the instant flour and set aside.

3. Preheat the oven to 350°F.

4. Heat a large nonstick sauté pan over medium-high heat, and add the olive oil. When it is hot, add the patties to the pan and cook for 3 minutes on the first side. Carefully flip the burgers over and cook for another 3 to 4 minutes on the other side. Place the burgers on a baking sheet, and bake in the oven for 10 minutes to cook through.

5. Meanwhile, brush the hamburger buns with the melted butter, and place them in the oven to warm, about 5 minutes.

6. In a medium mixing bowl, combine the mixed greens with enough vinaigrette to coat, and season lightly with salt and pepper.

7. To assemble: Place a burger on the bottom half of a bun, and top with one-quarter of the mixed greens and 1 tablespoon or more of the Cranberry Chutney. Place the top half of the bun on the burger. Repeat with the remaining ingredients. Cut the burgers in half, and serve immediately.

# TUNISIAN LAMB BURGER

4 burgers

I've spiced these lamb patties with caraway, coriander, and Aleppo pepper and then topped them with a carrot salad containing preserved lemon and harissa. Together with a cumin-scented mayo, these Tunisian-inspired ingredients make a lamb burger that you'll not soon forget.

1½ teaspoons caraway seeds, lightly crushed

1½ teaspoons coriander seeds, lightly crushed

1½ pounds ground lamb

1½ tablespoons ground Aleppo pepper (see Note)

1 teaspoon ground allspice

⅓ cup grated yellow onion

⅓ cup chopped fresh parsley leaves

1 tablespoon minced garlic

2 teaspoons kosher salt

2 tablespoons olive oil

8 hamburger buns

1 tablespoon unsalted butter, melted

½ cup mayonnaise, homemade (see page 309), or store-bought

1 teaspoon ground cumin

4 leaves butter lettuce

Thinly sliced red onion, for serving

Grated Carrot Salad (recipe follows), for serving

1. Heat a small skillet over medium-high heat. Add the caraway and coriander seeds and cook, stirring or tossing frequently, until aromatic, about 1 minute. Remove from the skillet and set aside to cool.

2. Transfer the seeds to a mixing bowl. Crumble in the lamb. Add the Aleppo pepper, allspice, onion, parsley, and garlic, and mix gently but thoroughly to combine. Cover the bowl with plastic wrap, and refrigerate it for at least 2 hours and up to overnight for the flavors to come together.

3. Add the salt to the lamb mixture, and mix gently to combine. Form into four 6-ounce patties, just a little over ½ inch thick.

4. Preheat the oven to 400°F.

5. Heat the olive oil in a 12-inch nonstick sauté pan over medium-high heat. Add the patties and cook until nicely browned and crusted on both sides, 4 to 6 minutes per side. Remove from the pan and set aside to rest for a few minutes.

6. Arrange the hamburger buns, cut sides up, on a baking sheet. Lightly brush both halves of the buns with the butter. Bake in the oven until slightly crisp, about 5 minutes. Remove from the oven and set aside to cool.

7. Combine the mayonnaise and the cumin in a small bowl, and stir to mix well.

8. To assemble: Place the hamburger buns on a clean work surface. Spread some of the cumin mayonnaise over the bottom half of a bun. Add a lettuce leaf, a lamb patty, some sliced onion, and some of the Grated Carrot Salad. Place the top half of the bun over the carrot salad. Repeat with the remaining ingredients, and serve.

Note: You can find Aleppo pepper at specialty food stores and at Middle Eastern markets. If you can't find it, you can substitute a mix of 1 tablespoon sweet paprika and ½ teaspoon ground cayenne.

# Grated Carrot Salad

1¼ cups

1 cup finely grated carrot (4 to 5 medium carrots)

1 tablespoon Classic Red Harissa (page 322),
  or sambal oelek or chili garlic sauce (see Note), or to taste

2 teaspoons freshly squeezed lemon juice

1 teaspoon minced preserved lemon rind

¼ teaspoon minced garlic

Salt, for seasoning

¼ cup pitted and chopped black olives

Place the carrot, harissa, lemon juice, preserved lemon, garlic, and a few pinches of salt in a small mixing bowl. Using a fork, toss to combine. Let the carrot marinate at room temperature for about 20 minutes. Then stir in the black olives and use immediately.

Note: Sambal oelek and chili garlic sauce can be found in specialty food stores or at your local Asian or Middle Eastern market.

# FRIED CLAMS WITH TARTAR SAUCE

4 servings

This East Coast favorite requires clam strips as an ingredient—not whole belly clams or soft-shell clams. And don't even think of using canned baby clams here. Clam strips come from large sea clams and are slices of the "foot"; they are largely available in New England. If you're not in the New England area, you can source them online, or feel free to make this sandwich using fresh shrimp.

Vegetable oil, for frying

1 pound clam strips, or 1 pound large shrimp, peeled and split lengthwise

One 12-ounce can evaporated milk

4 hot dog buns or other soft rolls, sliced open

4 tablespoons (½ stick) butter, melted

1½ cups cornmeal

½ cup masa harina (corn flour)

1½ teaspoons salt, plus more for seasoning

½ teaspoon cayenne pepper

½ teaspoon paprika

2 cups very thinly sliced baby lettuces or romaine

2 teaspoons extra-virgin olive oil

Freshly ground white pepper, for seasoning

About ½ cup Tartar Sauce (page 337)

Potato salad or potato chips, for serving

1. Pour enough vegetable oil into a large-size heavy pot or deep-fryer to a depth of 4 inches and heat until the temperature reaches 350°F.

2. Meanwhile, in a small bowl, combine the clam strips or shrimp with the evaporated milk. Refrigerate until ready to use.

3. Preheat a grill pan to high. Brush the cut sides of the buns with the melted butter. Grill the buns for about 1 minute on each side. Remove them from the grill and set aside.

4. In a mixing bowl, combine the cornmeal, masa harina, salt, cayenne, and paprika. Drain the clams. Working with one-third of the clams at a time, dredge them in the cornmeal mixture. Sift the clams to remove any excess cornmeal, and then fry them in the hot oil for 50 to 60 seconds, until golden. Remove the clams from the fryer and drain them on a paper-towel-lined plate. Repeat with the remaining clams.

5. In a small bowl, lightly toss the lettuce with the olive oil, and season with salt and white pepper.

6. To assemble: Spread about 2 tablespoons of the Tartar Sauce onto each hot dog bun, and dress with the greens. Mound the fried clams on top of the greens. Serve immediately, with potato salad or potato chips alongside, as desired.

Columbia Street Grinder,
see page 117

# Subs

## AND COUSINS

# FRIED OYSTER PO'BOY WITH JALAPEÑO MAYONNAISE AND AVOCADO

4 sandwiches

Oh, baby, the crispy fried "ersters," the salty bacon, and the creamy avocado all come together in this ultimate oyster sandwich. If you've ever wanted to re-create the experience of a fried oyster po'boy from New Orleans, save the flight—this is it!

1¼ cups buttermilk (see Note, page 64)

¼ cup your favorite Louisiana red hot sauce

¼ cup Emeril's Original Essence or Creole Seasoning (page 9)

4 dozen oysters, shucked and drained

1½ cups masa harina (corn flour)

1½ cups all-purpose flour

6 cups vegetable oil, for frying

Salt and freshly ground black pepper, to taste

Four 8-inch lengths po'boy bread (see Note),
    or French or Italian loaves, split lengthwise

3 tablespoons butter, melted

Jalapeño Mayo (page 311)

Shredded lettuce, for serving

1 medium tomato, thinly sliced

1 avocado, thinly sliced

8 to 12 strips bacon, cooked until crisp

1. Combine the buttermilk, hot sauce, and 2 tablespoons of the Essence in a medium mixing bowl, and stir to combine. Add the oysters and marinate for up to 30 minutes, refrigerated.

2. In a separate medium bowl, combine the masa harina, all-purpose flour, and remaining 2 tablespoons Essence, and stir to blend.

3. Heat the vegetable oil in a medium-size heavy pot or deep-fryer until the temperature reaches 360°F. Working in batches, remove the oysters from the buttermilk marinade and transfer them to the masa harina mixture. Dredge to coat, shaking to remove any excess breading. Cook the oysters in small batches in the hot oil until golden brown and crispy, 2 to 3 minutes. Remove with a slotted spoon and transfer to paper towels to drain. Season with salt and pepper, and set aside.

4. To assemble: Spread the bottom halves of the bread with the melted butter. Generously spread the top halves of the bread with Jalapeño Mayonnaise. Divide the oysters evenly among the bottom halves, followed by the lettuce, tomato, avocado, and bacon. Place the top halves of the bread over the fillings and press lightly. Cut each sandwich in half and serve immediately.

Note: Traditional New Orleans po'boy loaves are airy, long French breads. If you cannot find po'boy bread in your area, substitute any long Italian or French bread loaves that are not too dense. If the only bread you can find is very dense, consider pinching out the center doughy portions so that your po'boy is not overly bready.

# PANÉED VEAL HOAGIE WITH SMOTHERED MUSHROOMS AND ONIONS

4 hoagies

Panéed veal is a real treat—even for New Orleanians, for whom it is a fairly common menu item. Here the crisp-fried meat is dressed up with a simple mushroom and onion sauce. If you're not a fan of veal, substitute thinly sliced beef top round or sirloin, or thinly sliced pork or turkey cutlets. No matter which meat you choose, the secret to a cracker-crisp crust is to pound the meat very thin and then press the meat firmly into the breadcrumbs when breading. Be forewarned: this cooks very quickly, so have everything ready when you get to frying!

2 tablespoons olive oil

3 tablespoons unsalted butter

3 cups roughly chopped yellow onion

1¾ teaspoons kosher salt

½ teaspoon freshly ground black pepper

1 pound mixed mushrooms, such as button, cremini, and shiitake, stems trimmed or removed, caps wiped clean and thinly sliced

1½ tablespoons minced garlic

2 teaspoons all-purpose flour

1 cup beef stock or packaged low-sodium beef broth

1 tablespoon finely chopped fresh marjoram leaves

¾ cup buttermilk (see Note, page 64)

½ teaspoon cayenne pepper

2 cups Italian-style breadcrumbs

1 pound veal scaloppine

Peanut oil, for frying

Four 6-inch hoagie rolls, or sections of po'boy bread or
　　French or Italian bread, split lengthwise

Mayonnaise, homemade (see page 309), or store-bought

8 ounces sliced mozzarella or provolone cheese

1. Heat the olive oil in a large skillet over high heat. When it is hot, add 2 tablespoons of the butter, the onion, ¼ teaspoon of the salt, and ¼ teaspoon of the pepper. Sauté until the onion is soft and lightly golden around the edges, about 5 minutes. Add the mushrooms, ½ teaspoon of the salt, and ¼ teaspoon of the pepper and continue cooking, stirring occasionally, until the mushrooms are soft, have released their liquid, and are golden brown, 4 to 5 minutes. Add the remaining 1 tablespoon butter, the garlic, and the flour and cook, stirring, for 2 minutes. Stir in the stock and cook until thickened, 3 to 4 minutes. Stir in the marjoram, cover, and keep warm until you are ready to assemble the sandwiches.

2. Place the buttermilk, the remaining 1 teaspoon salt, and the cayenne in a medium bowl and stir to combine. Place the breadcrumbs in a second bowl. Position a large wire rack over a large baking sheet and set it aside.

3. Preheat the oven to 375°F.

4. Place 2 pieces of the veal between two sheets of plastic wrap, and using the smooth side of a meat mallet, pound to a thickness of about ⅛ inch. Cut each piece of meat into 2 or 3 smaller pieces so that it will fit on the bread. Repeat with the remaining slices of veal. Then transfer all the veal to the bowl with the buttermilk, turning to coat each slice. One at a time, remove the veal pieces, allowing the excess buttermilk to drip off, and then dredge them in the breadcrumbs, pressing the meat firmly into the crumbs so that they adhere well. Transfer the breaded cutlets to a large platter or baking sheet.

5. Pour peanut oil into a large skillet to a depth of ¾ inch, and heat it over medium-high heat. When the oil is hot but not smoking, fry the meat, in small batches to avoid overcrowding the skillet, until crisp and golden brown, 40 seconds to 1 minute. Transfer the cutlets to the wire rack to drain while you cook the remaining slices.

6. Place the bread, cut side down, on a baking sheet and toast it lightly in the oven, 2 to 3 minutes. Remove the bread, place an oven rack about 8 inches below the broiler unit, and turn the oven setting to broil. Line a large baking sheet with parchment paper.

7. To assemble: Spread each piece of bread with mayonnaise, and then place the bottom portions on the prepared baking sheet and set the top portions aside. Divide the meat evenly among the bottoms, spoon some of the mushroom sauce over the meat, and then top with the sliced cheese. Broil until the cheese is melted, about 2 minutes. Remove from the oven, top with the toasted top portions of the bread, and serve immediately, drizzled with additional sauce if desired.

# SMOKED SAUSAGE SANDWICHES WITH BEER-BRAISED ONIONS

4 sandwiches

Ante up, folks. This is *the* sandwich for poker night at your place. You get your cards in one hand and a sandwich in the other . . . And bet on the beer-braised onions—they're smokin'.

2 tablespoons unsalted butter, plus 4 tablespoons (½ stick),
    at room temperature
8 cups thinly sliced onion
¾ teaspoon salt
½ teaspoon freshly ground black pepper
One 12-ounce bottle American-style lager,
    such as Budweiser
1 pound smoked sausage
2 teaspoons vegetable oil
8 slices Muenster cheese
1 loaf French bread, about 22 inches long,
    cut into four 5½-inch sections, each split horizontally
Mayonnaise, homemade (see page 309), or store-bought
Whole-grain mustard
Spicy dill pickle slices

1. Melt the 2 tablespoons butter in a 10-inch skillet over medium-high heat. Mound the onion in the skillet and add the salt and pepper. Reduce the heat to medium-low and cook, stirring as needed, for 10 minutes, or until the onion is softened and lightly caramelized around the edges. Add the beer and cook for 25 minutes longer,

or until most of the liquid has evaporated and the onion is very soft and flavorful. Remove the skillet from the heat and allow the onion to cool slightly.

2. Cut the smoked sausage in lengths to fit the bread; then halve the sausage pieces lengthwise. Oil a grill pan with the vegetable oil and heat it over high heat. Add the sausages and grill until the casings are blistered and crisp and the sausages are heated through. Transfer the sausages to a plate and immediately lay the cheese slices on top, so that the cheese softens.

3. Butter the insides of the bread, using 1 tablespoon of the softened butter for each sandwich. In batches, add the bread to the grill pan, buttered side down, and cook until crisp, about 2 minutes. Transfer to a plate and spread mayonnaise on one side and mustard on the other. Add the sausages and cheese, mound with the onion, and garnish with pickles. Serve immediately.

# SPICY MEATLOAF PO'BOYS
# WITH SMOKED PROVOLONE

4 sandwiches

This sandwich was created for my friend Diane Sawyer as a special treat for her last day on *Good Morning America*. Diane is a meatloaf sandwich lover, and I tried my best to pull out all the stops on this one. You won't be sorry if you take the time to make the Spicy Meatloaf as called for here, but of course any leftover meatloaf can make for a mean sandwich . . .

1 cup mayonnaise, homemade (see page 309),
    or store-bought
1 teaspoon Emeril's Original Essence or
    Creole Seasoning (page 9)
1 teaspoon Tabasco sauce or other Louisiana red hot sauce
¼ teaspoon cayenne pepper
1 clove garlic, mashed to a paste with a fork
Four 4-inch sections po'boy bread or French or Italian bread
    (see Note, page 96)
Four to six ¾-inch-thick slices Spicy Meatloaf
    (recipe follows) or leftover meatloaf, warmed
8 slices smoked provolone cheese (about 1 ounce each)
Shredded lettuce, for serving (optional)
Thinly sliced tomato, for serving (optional)
Thinly sliced dill pickles or pickled peppers,
    for serving (optional)

1. Preheat the oven to 250°F.

2. In a small bowl, combine the mayonnaise, Essence, Tabasco, cayenne, and garlic, and stir to blend.

3. Cut the po'boy bread in half lengthwise and place, cut side down, on a baking sheet. Heat in the oven until just warmed through and lightly toasted, 3 to 4 minutes. (The bread should still be soft.) Remove from the oven, and raise the oven setting to broil. Position a rack as close as possible to the broiler.

4. Spread the cut sides of the bread liberally with the seasoned mayonnaise. Divide the sliced meatloaf evenly among the bottom halves of the bread, cutting the slices to fit the bread. Then top each of the meatloaf halves and each of the unfilled halves with 1 slice of cheese. Place on the baking sheet and broil until the cheese is melted and bubbly, 1 to 2 minutes. Remove from the oven and dress each sandwich with lettuce, tomato slices, and pickles or pickled peppers, as desired. Place the sandwich halves together and serve immediately.

## Spicy Meatloaf

6 servings

This kicked-up meatloaf is excellent on its own, served with mashed potatoes and green peas for a true comfort food experience, but watch out—sandwiches made with the leftovers are killer. You might even want to consider making two meatloaves, just to ensure that there will be leftovers the next day!

3 ounces thick-cut smoked bacon, diced

2 cups finely chopped onion

1 cup finely chopped celery

¼ cup finely chopped green bell pepper

¼ cup minced and seeded jalapeño pepper

    (about 2 medium peppers)

3 tablespoons minced garlic

1 teaspoon chopped fresh thyme leaves

1 tablespoon Emeril's Original Essence or

    Creole Seasoning (page 9)

1 teaspoon salt

2 teaspoons freshly ground black pepper

½ teaspoon cayenne pepper

¼ cup chopped green onion

2 tablespoons minced fresh parsley leaves

1½ pounds ground chuck (85% lean)

12 ounces fresh hot pork sausage

¾ cup coarse dry breadcrumbs,

    preferably homemade

2 eggs, beaten

¾ cup heavy cream

1 cup chili sauce

2 tablespoons dark brown sugar

2 teaspoons Worcestershire sauce

1. Cook the bacon in a large skillet over medium-high heat until it is very crisp and the fat has rendered, 8 to 10 minutes. Add the onion, celery, bell pepper, and jalapeño and cook, stirring frequently, until the vegetables are very soft and lightly caramelized, about 10 minutes. Add the garlic, thyme, Essence, salt, 1 teaspoon of the black pepper, and the cayenne, and cook for 2 minutes. Add the green onion and parsley, stir to combine, and transfer to a plate to cool.

2. Preheat the oven to 375°F.

3. In a large bowl, using your hands, gently crumble the ground beef and pork sausage into small pieces. Add the cooled vegetable mixture and the breadcrumbs to the meat. In a separate bowl, lightly whisk together the eggs and heavy cream; pour this over the meat. Working very gently and taking care not to overwork the meat, fold the ingredients together until thoroughly blended. Place the meat mixture into a small, shallow baking dish or a 1½-quart oval gratin dish, and shape it into a wide loaf.

4. In a small bowl, combine the chili sauce, dark brown sugar, Worcestershire, and remaining 1 teaspoon black pepper, and stir to blend. Pour the chili sauce mixture over the meatloaf and spread it so that the loaf is evenly coated. Bake the meatloaf, uncovered, until the center registers 160°F on an instant-read thermometer, about 1 hour. Remove it from the oven and allow it to cool briefly before slicing. Spoon off any accumulated fat drippings before serving, if desired.

# ROAST BEEF "DEBRIS" PO'BOY

6 servings

Everyone in New Orleans has their favorite po'boy. For some, it's fried oysters; some like grilled hot sausage; and for many, it is this—a pot roast stuffed with lots of garlic that's cooked until it's literally falling apart. The meltingly tender meat is then shredded and added back to the beefy pan drippings that soak into the po'boy bread like no one's business. Don't let the name scare you—the tiny bits of meat that fall into the drippings are the "debris" part, and it's certainly the best kind of debris I've ever heard of. Warning: bring a napkin.

1 boneless beef chuck roast (3 to 4 pounds)

10 cloves garlic, cut in half lengthwise

2 teaspoons salt

1 teaspoon freshly ground black pepper

2 tablespoons vegetable oil

2 cups beef stock or packaged low-sodium beef broth,
    plus more if necessary

Six 6-inch lengths po'boy bread or Italian or French bread
    (see Note, page 96)

Mayonnaise, homemade (see page 309), or store-bought

10 ounces provolone cheese, grated

Thinly shredded iceberg lettuce

Very thinly sliced tomatoes

Thinly sliced dill pickles

Louisiana red hot sauce (optional)

1. Using the tip of a sharp paring knife, make 20 evenly spaced small slits, about 1½ inches deep, all over the pot roast. Insert the garlic cloves as deep into the slits as possible. Season the roast on all sides with the salt and pepper.

2. Preheat the oven to 300°F.

3. Heat a 6-quart Dutch oven over high heat. Add the oil, and when it is hot, sear the meat until it is very well browned on all sides, 4 to 6 minutes per side (don't be afraid to let the roast get very brown—this is where a lot of the flavor comes from). Then carefully add the stock and cover the pot. Transfer the pot to the oven and cook, turning the meat once or twice during cooking, until the roast is falling-apart tender, 3 to 3½ hours. Check occasionally to make sure that there is always at least 1 inch of liquid in the bottom of the pot, adding water or additional stock as necessary.

4. Remove the roast from the oven and let it rest briefly. Increase the oven temperature to 375°F.

5. Using two forks, pull the meat apart into thin shreds, mixing the meat with the accumulated drippings in the bottom of the pot. Allow the meat to cool slightly and absorb the juices before making the po'boys. (The meat can be cooked and shredded up to 1 week in advance and refrigerated until ready to serve; if prepared in advance, it will need to be rewarmed—covered and in a low oven—before assembling the sandwiches.)

6. Halve the po'boy bread lengthwise, and spread both sides of the bread liberally with mayonnaise. Place the bottom halves of the bread on a baking sheet, and spoon the meat filling over them, drizzling it with extra drippings. Then top the meat with the grated provolone. Bake in the oven just until the cheese is melted, 2 to 3 minutes. Remove from the oven and top with lettuce, tomatoes, and pickles. Sprinkle with hot sauce, if desired, and top the po'boys with the top halves of the bread. Serve immediately.

# POOR MAN'S FRENCH FRY PO'BOY

4 sandwiches

This po'boy is really just that . . . a poor man's po'boy. This sandwich was born from the need to feed a family with a meager amount of leftover roast beef and a few potatoes. However, the combination of homemade French fries, roast beef gravy, and melted Swiss cheese happens to be one of New Orleans' most beloved po'boys, a real manly man's sandwich. Give it a try—you'll be a convert, too.

4 large russet or Kennebec potatoes
    (3 to 4 pounds),
    peeled and cut into ½-inch-wide x ½-inch-thick fries
3 tablespoons unsalted butter
5 tablespoons all-purpose flour
½ cup finely minced onion
2 tablespoons minced garlic
3½ cups beef stock or packaged
    low-sodium beef broth
¾ teaspoon freshly ground black pepper
1 cup chopped leftover roast beef,
    preferably homemade (see page 107)
Salt, to taste
Peanut oil, for frying
Four 6-inch lengths po'boy bread,
    or Italian or French bread (see Note, page 96)

Mayonnaise, homemade (see page 309),

   or store-bought

6 ounces sliced Swiss cheese

Hot sauce, for serving (optional)


1. Rinse the potato batons well under cool running water until the water runs clear. Then place them in a large bowl and cover with ice water. Refrigerate for at least 30 minutes and up to 2 days.

2. Meanwhile, make the roast beef gravy: Melt the butter in a medium saucepan over medium-high heat and whisk in the flour. Cook, stirring continuously, until a milk chocolate–colored roux is formed, 4 to 6 minutes. Add the onion and garlic and cook until soft, 2 to 4 minutes. Whisk in the beef stock, little by little, and bring the sauce to a boil. Stir in the pepper, reduce the heat to a simmer, and cook until the sauce has reduced to a gravy consistency, 15 to 20 minutes. Stir in the roast beef and season with salt. Cover the gravy and set it aside up to 1 week, refrigerated, until you are ready to serve the po'boys.

3. Fill a deep 5-quart pot or Dutch oven fitted with a candy or deep-frying thermometer, or an electric deep-fryer, with peanut oil to a depth of 4 inches. Make sure that you have at least 3 inches of space between the top of the oil and the top of the pot, as the fries will bubble up when they are added. Heat the oil over medium-low heat until the thermometer registers 325°F.

4. Drain the ice water from the potatoes, wrap them in a clean dishcloth, and thoroughly pat them dry. Fry the potatoes in small batches in the hot oil, stirring them occasionally, until they are soft and limp and are beginning to turn blond, 6 to 8 minutes. Using a slotted spoon or a skimmer, carefully transfer the potatoes to paper towels to drain. Let them rest for at least 10 minutes and up to 2 hours. Unless you are going to proceed, turn off the heat.

5. When you are ready to serve the po'boys, set the oven to broil and reheat the frying oil to 350°F. (Reheat the gravy if necessary.) Working in batches, return the potatoes

to the hot oil and fry again, stirring frequently, until they are golden brown, puffed, and crisp, 2 to 3 minutes. Transfer the fries to a paper-towel-lined platter and season them with salt.

6. Halve the po'boy bread lengthwise and spread both sides generously with mayonnaise. Place the bottom halves of the bread on a baking sheet, and divide the fries evenly among them. Spoon some of the gravy over the fries, and then top with the Swiss cheese. Place the baking sheet in the oven and broil until the cheese is melted, 1 to 2 minutes. Remove from the oven and top with the remaining bread. Serve immediately, with additional gravy for sopping and with hot sauce if desired.

# LEMONGRASS CHICKEN BANH MI

4 sandwiches

New Orleanians have wholeheartedly embraced banh mi sandwiches, which are basically the Vietnamese equivalent of our beloved po'boys. Many bakeries in New Orleans now make perfect banh mi bread, which, like po'boy bread, is crisp on the outside with a light and airy inside. My version here is filled with broiled lemongrass-scented chicken and topped with pickled carrots and lots of fresh herbs (don't forget the jalapeños!), a true party of flavors. The chicken needs to marinate for at least four hours, so you may want to consider preparing it a day in advance and letting it marinate overnight. Then, the next day it's one-two-three to put these together.

## Marinade and chicken

2 to 3 lemongrass stalks, bottom 6 inches thinly sliced crosswise
   (about 2 generous tablespoons)

1 tablespoon minced garlic

1 tablespoon light brown sugar

1 fresh red chile, such as cayenne, minced,
   or ¼ teaspoon crushed red pepper

½ teaspoon ground coriander

¼ teaspoon kosher salt, plus more for seasoning

1½ tablespoons Vietnamese fish sauce

¼ teaspoon soy sauce

3 tablespoons vegetable oil

6 boneless, skinless chicken thighs (about 1½ pounds)

Four 8-inch banh mi breads, or four 8-inch sections French bread

Mayonnaise, homemade (see page 309), or store-bought

Sriracha sauce, to taste

1 cup thinly sliced red cabbage

Quick Pickled Carrots (recipe follows)

1 medium cucumber, thinly sliced on the diagonal

1 to 2 jalapeños, thinly sliced crosswise, with seeds

Fresh basil, mint, and cilantro leaves, for garnish

1. Prepare the chicken: Combine the lemongrass, garlic, brown sugar, red chile, coriander, and salt in a mortar, and using a pestle, pound to form a paste. Stir in the fish sauce, soy sauce, and oil. Transfer the marinade to a medium nonreactive bowl.

2. Using a sharp knife, trim off and discard any excess fat or remaining cartilage from the chicken thighs. Dip the chicken pieces in the lemongrass mixture, turning to coat on both sides, and then nestle the pieces down into any remaining marinade. Cover and refrigerate for at least 4 hours and up to overnight.

3. When you are ready to cook the chicken, remove it from the refrigerator and allow it to sit at room temperature for up to 30 minutes.

4. Position an oven rack as close to the broiler unit as possible and preheat the broiler.

5. Transfer the chicken pieces to a foil-lined baking sheet and season them lightly with kosher salt. Broil the chicken until just cooked through, 4 to 6 minutes. Remove from the broiler, set aside to cool briefly, and then slice the chicken into thin strips.

6. To assemble the sandwiches: Halve the bread lengthwise and spread both halves generously with mayonnaise. Drizzle Sriracha sauce on the upper pieces of bread, to taste. Divide the chicken strips evenly among the bottom portions of bread, and then top them with the sliced cabbage, pickled carrots, cucumber slices, and jalapeños to taste. Tear any large basil leaves into pieces and sprinkle them over the sandwiches,

along with the mint and cilantro. Top with the remaining bread, cut the sandwiches in half, and serve.

## Quick Pickled Carrots

¾ cup pickled carrots for 4 to 6 sandwiches

1 cup rice vinegar

3 tablespoons sugar

1 fresh red chile, such as cayenne, thinly sliced crosswise,
   or ¼ teaspoon crushed red pepper

¼ teaspoon salt

2 large carrots, thinly sliced on the diagonal

1. Combine the vinegar, sugar, chile, and salt in a medium saucepan, and bring to a boil over medium heat, stirring until the sugar is dissolved. Remove from the heat and set aside to cool briefly.

2. Place the carrots in a heatproof nonreactive bowl, and pour the warm pickling liquid over them. Set aside for at least 1 hour before using, or cover and refrigerate for up to several days.

# COLUMBIA STREET GRINDER

4 sandwiches

I have many fond memories of eating grinders back home, but none that stick out in my mind more than the ones I'd find on Columbia Street in Fall River, Massachusetts. Though Columbia Street can't be matched, I've tried my best to devise a recipe that comes close, and I think this one hits the mark.

Four 6-inch loaves Portuguese stick bread, or Italian or French loaves

Balsamic-Herb Vinaigrette (page 329)

8 ounces sliced provolone cheese

8 ounces sliced mortadella

8 ounces sliced spicy ham, such as capicola

8 ounces sliced salami

1 large ripe tomato, cut into eight ¼-inch-thick slices

12 thin onion slices

12 jarred hot or sweet cherry peppers, drained and roughly chopped

2 cups torn green-leaf lettuce

1. Cut the loaves of bread in half lengthwise, and arrange them in a single layer, cut sides up. Liberally brush the bread with the vinaigrette. On the bottom half of each loaf, evenly layer one-quarter of the provolone, followed by one-quarter of the mortadella, one-quarter of the spicy ham, and one-quarter of the salami. Top with 2 slices of tomatos and 3 slices of onion. Divide the cherry peppers among the sandwiches. Stir the vinaigrette and generously drizzle it over the onion and tomato.

2. In a small bowl, toss the torn lettuce with some of the remaining vinaigrette. Divide the lettuce among the 4 sandwiches, top with the other halves of the bread, and serve.

# PHILLY CHEESESTEAK, MY WAY

4 sandwiches

Most of us don't have a flat-top griddle in our house to make a perfectly authentic-tasting Philly cheesesteak. But I have a great way to mimic the method for this iconic sandwich: Griddle the onions and peppers in a cast-iron skillet instead, and then keep them warm until you're ready to slather them on top of the meat and cheese. Just as you're filling the sandwich, it all melts together—with a few cherry peppers for a twist. Rib-eye steaks will give you the tenderest meat, but you can use sirloin or top round as well.

Two 1-pound rib-eye steaks

Four 8-inch sections French bread or po'boy bread

8 slices provolone cheese (about 8 ounces)

8 slices good-quality American cheese (about 8 ounces)

¼ cup vegetable oil

4 cups small-diced onion

2 cups sliced green bell pepper

2 teaspoons salt

¾ teaspoon freshly ground black pepper

¼ cup roughly chopped jarred cherry (pimento) peppers or Peppadew peppers

1. Wrap each steak individually in plastic wrap, place them in the freezer, and freeze for about 3 hours; this will make it easier to slice the meat.

2. Remove 1 steak from the freezer and use a very sharp knife to slice it as thin as you can, discarding any pockets of fat. Set aside, and repeat with the other steak.

3. Preheat the oven to 300°F.

4. Slice open the French bread, and set it aside on a large baking sheet.

5. Arrange the cheese in four overlapping piles on a large serving platter, alternating slices of provolone and American.

6. Heat 2 tablespoons of the olive oil in a large cast-iron skillet set over medium-high heat. Add the onion and bell pepper, 1 teaspoon of the salt, and ¼ teaspoon of the black pepper. Cook, stirring occasionally, until the onion is lightly caramelized and tender, about 8 minutes. Stir in the cherry peppers, and then transfer the onion and peppers to the same baking sheet with the bread, and place in the oven to keep warm while you cook the steak.

7. Making 2 sandwiches at a time, increase the heat under the skillet to high and add 1 tablespoon oil. Add half the steak slices, season them with ½ teaspoon salt and ¼ teaspoon pepper, and cook without stirring until most of the meat has browned on one side, about 1 minute. Stir the meat, and then divide it into two cylindrical portions. Lay a shingled pile of cheese over each pile of meat. Remove the baking sheet from the oven and spoon one-quarter of the onion and peppers over each cheese-topped meat pile. Continue to cook in the skillet, undisturbed, for 1 minute longer, or until the cheese begins to melt from the heat of the vegetables. Using a large spatula, transfer each of the meat portions to a bottom half of the bread. Set the 2 filled sandwiches on a small baking sheet and place them in the oven to keep warm. Wipe the skillet clean and repeat to make the other 2 sandwiches.

# CHORIZO AND SAUTÉED PEPPER SANDWICH WITH LEMONY OLIVE OIL–CILANTRO DRIZZLE

4 sandwiches

This sausage and pepper sandwich is inspired by my Portuguese roots: bell pepper, onion, garlic, cilantro, lemon, paprika, and chorizo. How can you go wrong with that? But what really makes this sandwich special is the intense sauce. Wow! If you're lucky enough to find Portuguese stick bread in your area, that's what I suggest. Otherwise, a nice French loaf or a rustic bread that's not too dense will do just fine.

¼ cup freshly squeezed lemon juice

1 to 3 fresh red chiles, such as cayenne, Thai, or red jalapeño, stemmed and chopped

1 tablespoon finely chopped garlic

1½ teaspoons sweet paprika

½ teaspoon hot pimentón (hot smoked Spanish paprika)

½ teaspoon salt, plus more for seasoning

½ cup chopped fresh cilantro leaves

⅓ cup plus 3 tablespoons Portuguese or Spanish extra-virgin olive oil

1 red bell pepper, julienned (about 2 cups)

1 yellow bell pepper, julienned (about 2 cups)

½ yellow onion, julienned (about 1 cup)

Freshly ground black pepper, for seasoning

1½ pounds smoked chorizo sausage (or other spicy sausage,

   such as linguiça or spicy Italian), cut into 6-inch lengths and

   halved lengthwise (8 pieces)

Four 6-inch loaves Portuguese stick bread,

   or four 6-inch sections French bread,

   split and lightly toasted

1. Combine the lemon juice, chile pepper(s), garlic, paprika, pimentón, salt, and ¼ cup of the cilantro leaves in a blender, and puree. With the motor running, slowly drizzle in the ⅓ cup olive oil to form an emulsion, and continue to blend for 1 minute, until the mixture is uniform. Transfer to a small serving bowl and stir in the remaining ¼ cup cilantro. Set aside.

2. Heat 2 tablespoons of the olive oil in a 12-inch sauté pan over medium-high heat. Add the bell peppers, onion, a few generous pinches of salt, and a pinch of black pepper, and cook until the vegetables are lightly browned and soft, stirring occasionally, 5 to 6 minutes. Remove from the pan and set aside on a large plate.

3. Add the remaining 1 tablespoon olive oil to the sauté pan. Add the sausage, in batches if necessary, and cook until browned and blistered, 2 to 3 minutes per side. Transfer to the plate with the peppers and onion.

4. Arrange the toasted bread on a clean work surface. Place 2 sausage pieces on each bottom half of the bread. Drizzle with 1 to 2 tablespoons of the sauce. Divide the pepper-and-onion mixture among the 4 sandwiches, and drizzle a bit more of the sauce on top. Gently press the top halves of the bread over the filling, and serve immediately.

Grilled Spinach and Artichoke Dip Sandwich,
see pages 141–142

# PRESSED AND GRILLED

# SMOKY GRILLED PIMENTO CHEESE

I generous pint pimento cheese spread, about 12 sandwiches

This classic Southern spread makes a mean grilled cheese! A hint of sweet pimentón gives this version a unique smoky flavor that is surprisingly at home when sandwiched between two pieces of quickly pan-crisped white bread.

12 ounces extra-sharp yellow cheddar, coarsely grated,
   at room temperature

Two 4-ounce jars diced pimentos, well drained

6 to 8 tablespoons mayonnaise, preferably homemade
   (see page 309), or more to taste

1 tablespoon grated red onion

½ teaspoon kosher salt

½ teaspoon sweet pimentón (smoked Spanish paprika)

¼ teaspoon Crystal or your favorite Louisiana red hot sauce

¼ teaspoon cayenne pepper

2 pinches sugar

About 24 slices White Sandwich Bread (page 303),
   or as needed (see Note)

Butter, at room temperature, as needed

1. Combine the cheese, pimentos, mayonnaise, onion, salt, pimentón, hot sauce, cayenne, and sugar in a medium mixing bowl, and stir until the cheese is still distinct but has begun to meld with the mayonnaise. Taste, and adjust the seasoning if necessary. Cover the pimento cheese and refrigerate until slightly firm, at least 2 hours and up to several days in advance.

2. When you are ready to make the sandwiches, heat a nonstick skillet over medium-high heat.

3. For each sandwich, spread a generous 2 tablespoons of the pimento cheese evenly between 2 slices of bread. Spread the outsides of the sandwich with softened butter. Cook in the skillet just until lightly golden on both sides, about 1 minute per side. Repeat with any remaining sandwiches and serve immediately.

Note: Any leftover pimento cheese will keep for up to several days in the refrigerator and is wonderful slathered on burgers, served with crackers, or used as a dip for vegetable crudités.

# THE CUBAN

4 sandwiches

It is hard to improve on a good Cuban sandwich, but of course I had to try. This one's filled with spice-rubbed pork and slathered with a quick-mix garlic saffron mayo (secret: the sandwich is still good without the saffron). With mortadella and sliced onions too, it's extreme.

2 teaspoons ground cumin

1 teaspoon kosher salt

1 teaspoon ground coriander

½ teaspoon freshly ground black pepper

Grated zest of 1 lime

1 pound pork tenderloin, trimmed of any fat or tough membranes

1 tablespoon olive oil

4 pinches saffron threads (optional)

1 teaspoon water, if using saffron

1 cup mayonnaise, homemade (page 309), or store-bought

1 tablespoon minced garlic

1 loaf Cuban or French bread, about 24 inches long

4 thin slices ham (about 4 ounces)

4 thin slices mortadella (about 4 ounces)

½ cup thinly sliced onion rounds

8 slices dill pickle "stackers"

8 thin slices Swiss cheese (about 8 ounces)

4 tablespoons (½ stick) unsalted butter

1. Position an oven rack in the center and preheat the oven to 400°F.

2. In a small bowl, combine the cumin, salt, coriander, black pepper, and lime zest, and stir to mix well; season the tenderloin with the spice mixture.

3. Heat the olive oil in a 12-inch ovenproof skillet over high heat. Add the pork and sear it on all sides, about 5 minutes total. Transfer the skillet to the oven and roast for about 15 minutes, or until the thickest part of the tenderloin registers 145°F on an instant-read thermometer. Transfer the pork to a small cutting board, let it rest for at least 10 minutes, and then slice it crosswise into ¼-inch-thick slices.

4. If using, crumble the saffron into a small bowl. Add the water and let sit for about 5 minutes.

5. Place the mayonnaise in a small bowl. Add the saffron-water mixture, if using, and the garlic, and stir to combine.

6. Using a serrated knife, halve the loaf of bread lengthwise. Remove and discard some of the dense bready portion from one side, leaving about ½ inch of thickness. Leave the other half intact.

7. Generously spread the mayonnaise along both halves of the loaf. On the bottom half, layer the ham, mortadella, and pork tenderloin. Spread an even layer of sliced onion on top of the pork; then layer the pickle slices and Swiss cheese. Top with the other half of the bread, and press to close. Cut the loaf into 4 sandwiches.

8. Heat a medium nonstick skillet or griddle over medium heat, and add 1 tablespoon of the butter. Place 1 sandwich in the skillet and firmly press the top of the sandwich using a large metal spatula or a weighted sandwich press. Cook until browned, about 3 minutes. Using the spatula, turn the sandwich over and cook for 3 minutes longer, or until golden brown, pressing with the spatula to flatten it. Remove to a plate and keep warm.

9. Repeat with the remaining sandwiches and butter. Serve the sandwiches warm.

# GRILLED IDIAZÁBAL CHEESE WITH QUINCE PASTE, PEARS, AND WALNUT BUTTER

4 sandwiches

This sandwich is the quintessential Spanish snack. Idiazábal is a Spanish smoked sheep's-milk cheese, made in the Navarre region. Its flavor is nutty and smoky with slight hints of dried fruit. It pairs well with quince paste, also known as *dulce de Membrillo*, which is sold in specialty markets by the pound or in small containers. Quince has a very hard, dense flesh and an astringent flavor and therefore is almost never eaten raw. But once cooked, the fruit is sweet, with an almost floral flavor. Here you have quince paste combined with fresh pears and a creamy walnut butter. It's a cheese plate and sandwich all in one.

1 cup walnut halves

4 tablespoons (½ stick) unsalted butter, at room temperature

¼ teaspoon sea salt

8 slices German dark wheat bread or pumpernickel bread (see page 295)

4 ounces quince paste

6 ounces Idiazábal cheese, thinly sliced (or substitute Manchego cheese)

1 Bosc pear, thinly sliced (preferably on a mandoline)

1. Preheat the oven to 350°F.

2. Place the walnuts on a small baking sheet and bake until lightly toasted and fragrant, 7 to 10 minutes. Set aside until completely cool.

3. In a food processor or a blender, process the walnuts until almost smooth, about 1½ minutes. Add the butter and the sea salt and process for another 30 seconds, just to combine.

4. Spread 1 tablespoon of the walnut butter over each slice of bread. Divide the quince paste among 4 slices of the bread, then lay the cheese slices on top of the quince paste. Shingle about 8 slices of the pear over the cheese, and top with the remaining 4 slices of bread.

5. Heat a panini maker to medium-high, or heat a grill pan over medium-high heat. Cook the sandwiches, in batches if necessary, until the bread is crisp and the cheese has melted, about 4 minutes. Cut the sandwiches diagonally in halves or quarters, and serve immediately.

# GRILLED TRUFFLED CHEESE SANDWICHES WITH PROSCIUTTO AND MUSHROOMS

*6 sandwiches*

Truffled cheese and prosciutto transform an ordinary grilled ham and cheese sandwich into something outrageous. You can buy truffled cheese at a local cheese shop, gourmet market, or online. There really is no substitute.

2 cups grated Sottocenere cheese or other truffled cheese
    (about 8 ounces)
1 cup grated Fontina cheese (about 4 ounces)
Twelve 4 x 5-inch slices rustic Italian bread
12 thin slices prosciutto (about 7 ounces)
2 ounces cremini mushrooms, wiped clean
    and very thinly sliced (about 1 cup)
2 medium tomatoes, cut into 12 thin slices
6 tablespoons olive oil

1. In a medium mixing bowl, combine the cheeses and set aside.

2. Lay 6 slices of the bread on a clean work surface. Carefully fold 2 slices of prosciutto onto each, making sure that the prosciutto does not hang over the edges. Divide the mushrooms evenly over the prosciutto; then top with the sliced tomatoes and the cheese mixture. Place the remaining slices of bread on top.

3. Brush one side of each sandwich with about 1½ teaspoons of the olive oil.

4. Heat a grill pan over medium heat. When it is hot, place 2 sandwiches, olive oil side down, onto the pan. Brush the exposed side of the sandwiches with 1

tablespoon of the remaining olive oil. Use a grill press or another heavy pan to weight down the sandwiches. Cook the sandwiches for 2½ to 3 minutes, or until golden brown grill marks have formed and the cheese is beginning to melt. Turn to the other side and cook for another 2½ to 3 minutes, until the bread is crispy and the cheese is melted. Remove from the grill pan and cut the sandwiches in half diagonally. Cook the rest of the sandwiches in the same manner.

# GRILLED PEANUT BUTTER, BANANA, AND HONEY

4 sandwiches

You don't know what you've been missing. So long, jelly! Talk about melt-in-your mouth goodness. Hey, try it for a twist on breakfast for a protein-potassium-power punch. Or join the kids later and enjoy it as an afternoon snack.

8 slices Honey Whole Wheat Bread (page 283)

½ cup creamy peanut butter

2 ripe bananas, sliced into ¼-inch-thick rounds

2 tablespoons honey

2 tablespoons unsalted butter, melted

1. Place the bread on a clean work surface. Spread 1 tablespoon of peanut butter over each slice of bread. Divide the banana rounds equally among 4 of the slices, and drizzle 1½ teaspoons of the honey over each banana-topped slice. Top with the 4 remaining slices of bread. Using half of the melted butter, brush one side of each sandwich.

2. Heat a 12-inch sauté pan over medium-high heat. When it is hot, lower the temperature to medium. Place 2 sandwiches in the pan, buttered side down, and cook until crisp and browned, 1 to 2 minutes. Brush the tops of the sandwiches with some of the remaining melted butter. Turn the sandwiches over and cook the other side for another 1 to 2 minutes. Remove, and repeat with the remaining sandwiches. Slice the sandwiches in half diagonally, and serve immediately.

# DUCK CONFIT PANINI

6 sandwiches

You do not need to make duck confit from scratch for this recipe; you can buy it at your local gourmet shop or online. Same goes for the truffle butter. Be warned: This may be the most decadent sandwich in the book— and let me tell you, it's worth it! You won't be able to stop at just one.

3 confit duck legs (see Note)

1 pound oyster mushrooms, stems trimmed off, caps wiped clean and
   cut into bite-size pieces

1 tablespoon fresh thyme leaves

3 ounces truffle butter (see Note)

½ teaspoon sea salt

¼ teaspoon freshly ground black pepper

6 soft ciabatta rolls or panini rolls, cut in half

8 ounces sheep's-milk raclette cheese (or Gruyère or Emmenthaler), grated

1. Heat a large sauté pan over medium heat. Add the duck legs, skin side down, and cook for 4 to 6 minutes, until the skin is very crispy and the fat has begun to render out. Turn the legs over and continue to cook until they are golden brown, 3 to 4 minutes. Transfer the legs to a platter and set aside.

2. Raise the heat under the sauté pan to medium-high, and add half the oyster mushrooms, half the thyme, 1 tablespoon of the truffle butter, ¼ teaspoon of the salt, and ⅛ teaspoon of the pepper. Cook for 2 to 3 minutes, until the mushrooms are golden brown. Transfer the mushrooms to a plate and cook the remaining mushrooms in the same manner. Set the mushrooms aside.

3. Preheat the oven to 200°F. Preheat a panini press or heat a grill pan over medium-high heat.

4. Pull the meat and skin from the duck legs and chop it roughly (discard the bones). Divide the meat evenly among the bottom halves of the rolls; then top with the mushrooms and sprinkle with the grated cheese. Spread the inside of the top half of each roll with about 1 teaspoon of the truffle butter, and place on top of the cheese.

5. Cook 2 sandwiches at a time in the panini press for 2 to 3 minutes, or according to the manufacturer's directions, until golden and crisp and the cheese has melted. (If using a grill pan, grill the sandwiches, weighted with a press or other heavy pan, until golden and crisp on both sides, about 3 minutes each side.) Transfer them to a platter and place in the oven to keep warm. Repeat with the remaining sandwiches. Slice the sandwiches in half and serve immediately.

Note: Duck confit and truffle butter can be sourced online at D'Artagnan, or purchased at your local gourmet market and at some upscale butcher shops.

# GRILLED SPINACH AND ARTICHOKE DIP SANDWICH

8 sandwiches

The bite is cheesy, creamy, and delicious all at once. No chips needed here. Who would have thought you could get all that you love about a dip in a sandwich? But folks, you'll have to get this spread between the bread ASAP—they'll be coming at you from all angles for this one.

4 strips bacon, chopped

4 tablespoons (½ stick) unsalted butter,
    plus 4 tablespoons (½ stick), at room temperature

1 cup chopped onion

1 tablespoon minced garlic

¾ teaspoon salt

½ teaspoon freshly ground black pepper

¼ teaspoon crushed red pepper

18 ounces canned or jarred marinated artichoke hearts,
    drained and chopped

Two 9- or 10-ounce bags prewashed spinach

8 ounces Brie cheese, cut into ¼-inch cubes

4 ounces Monterey Jack cheese, grated

¼ cup grated Parmigiano-Reggiano cheese

16 slices White Sandwich Bread (page 303)

1. Cook the bacon in a medium skillet over medium heat until crisp; remove the bacon with a slotted spoon and set it aside on a paper towel to drain.

2. Discard all but 1 tablespoon of the bacon fat remaining in the skillet. Add the 4 tablespoons butter, and when it has melted, add the onion, garlic, salt, black

pepper, and crushed red pepper. Cook, stirring as needed, until the onion is very soft, about 10 minutes. Add the artichokes and cook for 2 minutes longer. Add 1 bag of spinach and cook until wilted, about 2 minutes; then add the second bag and cook, stirring as needed, for 4 minutes, until the spinach is tender and the flavors have blended. Remove from the heat.

3. Set a strainer over a bowl, and add the spinach-artichoke mixture to it. Allow the excess liquid to drain, about 5 minutes.

4. In a medium mixing bowl, combine the three cheeses. Then add the warm spinach mixture and stir until nicely combined and the cheese has begun to melt. Stir in the bacon.

5. To assemble: Evenly spread a packed ½ cup of filling between 2 slices of bread. Butter each side of the sandwich with about 1 teaspoon of the softened butter. Repeat with the remaining ingredients.

6. Heat a skillet or grill pan over medium heat. Cook the sandwiches, in batches, until they are browned on each side and the filling is warmed through, about 6 minutes. Cut the sandwiches, in half, and serve immediately.

# SPICY EGGPLANT WITH MOZZARELLA AND BASIL

4 sandwiches

If you weren't an eggplant lover before, you will be now! The key is to let the eggplant sit in a flavorful marinade. When you bite into the crispy bread, you'll be immediately seduced by the creamy eggplant and stretchy mozzarella. And then the whole thing comes together with an over-the-top minty-basil herbaceous pop. Wow.

¾ cup olive oil, plus more for brushing

¾ cup extra-virgin olive oil (see Note)

4 to 6 fresh red hot chiles, such as cayenne or Thai bird, stems removed

2 tablespoons plus 2 teaspoons minced garlic

2 to 4 large canned anchovy fillets

¼ cup nonpareil capers, drained, rinsed, and chopped

¼ cup finely chopped fresh mint leaves

1¾ to 2 pounds eggplant, stemmed and cut into ½-inch-thick rounds

Kosher salt, for seasoning

Freshly ground black pepper, for seasoning

8 slices rustic Italian bread

1 cup loosely packed fresh basil leaves

8 ounces buffalo or regular fresh mozzarella, cut into ¼-inch-thick slices

1. Place the olive oil, extra-virgin olive oil, chiles, garlic, and anchovies in a blender or food processor and blend until smooth. Transfer to a small bowl, and stir in the capers and mint leaves. Set the marinade aside.

2. Position an oven rack as close to the broiler element as possible and preheat the broiler.

3. Season the eggplant slices with salt on both sides, and arrange them on a wire rack positioned over a baking sheet. Let the eggplant drain for 30 minutes.

4. Rinse the eggplant slices briefly under cool water and pat them dry with paper towels. Generously brush both sides of the eggplant with olive oil. Arrange the slices in a single layer on a clean baking sheet; season both sides with kosher salt and black pepper. Transfer to the oven and broil until nicely browned, turning the eggplant over and rotating the baking sheet midway through cooking, 10 to 12 minutes total. Remove from the oven and set aside to cool briefly.

5. Using the same pastry brush, stir the reserved marinade and liberally brush some over one side of each eggplant slice, making sure to coat it well. Carefully transfer some of the eggplant, in one layer, to a small mixing bowl, placing the brushed side down. Brush the other side with marinade. Add another layer of eggplant, and repeat until all of the eggplant slices and marinade are used. Cover with plastic wrap and set aside to marinate for 2 to 4 hours at room temperature. Occasionally spoon some of the marinade that has gathered at the bottom of the bowl over the top.

6. To assemble: Lay 4 slices of the bread on a clean work surface, and arrange the basil leaves in a single layer to cover each slice, 3 to 4 leaves per slice. Remove the eggplant from the marinade with a slotted spoon, allowing any excess oil to drip back into the bowl, and divide the eggplant among the slices. Drain some of the solids from the marinade, spoon them over the eggplant, and season with salt and pepper. Divide the mozzarella slices evenly over the eggplant, and then place the remaining slices of bread on top. Lightly brush the bread with some of the remaining oil in the bowl (it is not necessary to oil the bottom slice).

7. Heat a panini maker to medium-high, or preheat a grill pan over medium-high heat. Cook the sandwiches, in batches if necessary, until crisp and the cheese has melted, 5 to 6 minutes. Cut each sandwich in half, and serve immediately.

Note: Using a combination of regular and extra-virgin olive oil gives the right balance of olive flavor for this marinade and is more cost-conscious than going with extra-virgin all the way.

# ARTICHOKE, SALAMI, AND FONTINA PANINI

6 sandwiches

Cheesy, salty, sour, crusty, and sweet with olive oil goodness. What a combination for a sandwich—especially one hot off the press!

Twelve ½-inch-thick slices ciabatta or other rustic white Italian bread

1 recipe Balsamic-Herb Vinaigrette (page 329)

6 ounces sliced Fontina cheese

Two 6.5-ounce jars marinated artichoke hearts, drained and sliced

4 ounces thinly sliced Genoa salami

1. Arrange the bread on a clean work surface and liberally brush the vinaigrette over each slice. Layer the Fontina, artichokes, and salami evenly on 6 of the slices. Top with the remaining slices of bread.

2. Preheat a panini press or heat a grill, large skillet, or grill pan over medium heat.

3. Cook the sandwiches in the panini press until the bread is golden brown and the cheese is melted, 6 to 8 minutes. (If using a grill pan or skillet, grill the sandwiches, pressing on them with a large spatula or the bottom of a small heavy saucepan, until golden on both sides.) Cut the panini in half, and serve.

Porchetta with Dandelion Greens,
see pages 161–163

# OPEN-FACE

# SPICY TUNA POKE

12 sandwiches, about 6 servings

My love for poke came from frequent trips to Hawaii with my buddy Sam Choy; *poke* basically means marinated raw, seared, or cooked seafood. There are tons of different marinades out there, but the one I like best is inspired by a spicy tuna roll.

¼ cup mayonnaise, homemade (see page 309), or store-bought

1 tablespoon plus 1 teaspoon soy sauce

1 tablespoon plus 1 teaspoon toasted sesame oil

1 tablespoon spicy chili sauce or paste (such as Sriracha or sambal oelek)

¾ teaspoon sea salt, plus more for seasoning

¾ cup peeled, seeded, and ¼-inch-diced cucumber

½ cup finely chopped red onion

1½ pounds sushi-grade tuna, cut into ¼-inch dice

12 slices sourdough sandwich bread

Olive oil, for brushing

Freshly ground black pepper, for seasoning

1 ripe avocado, peeled, pitted, and thinly sliced

2 tablespoons chopped fresh cilantro leaves, for garnish

1 large sheet seasoned nori, shredded into thin strips, for garnish

1. Preheat the oven to 400°F.

2. In a medium mixing bowl, whisk together the mayonnaise, soy sauce, sesame oil, chili sauce, and ¾ teaspoon sea salt. Add the cucumber, red onion, and tuna. Using a rubber spatula, gently stir together to evenly coat. Cover the tuna poke with plastic wrap and place it in the refrigerator until ready to use.

3. Arrange the slices of bread in a single layer on two baking sheets, and brush them lightly with olive oil. Season the bread with generous pinches of salt and pepper, and toast in the oven until crisp, about 10 minutes. Remove from the oven and set aside to cool.

4. To assemble: Arrange about 3 slices of avocado in a single layer on top of each slice of toast. Top with ¼ cup of the poke, and season lightly with salt. Garnish with the cilantro and the nori. Serve immediately.

# PORK RILLETTE ON PUMPERNICKEL WITH WATERCRESS AND FIG VINAIGRETTE

8 servings (about 3 halves per person)

The filling for this sandwich is buttery, luscious, and smooth. It may be everything you're trying to avoid, but this time, indulge yourself.

2 tablespoons unsalted butter, plus 4 tablespoons (½ stick)
    at room temperature

⅔ cup chopped shallot

2 tablespoons chopped garlic

¼ teaspoon salt, plus more for seasoning

½ teaspoon freshly ground black pepper,
    plus more for seasoning

¼ cup cognac

Confit Pork (recipe follows)

¼ cup chopped fresh parsley leaves

1 bunch watercress or arugula, rinsed and spun dry

Fig Vinaigrette (page 332)

12 slices pumpernickel bread (see page 295)

Whole-grain mustard, such as Pommery

½ cup cornichons, finely chopped

1. Melt the 2 tablespoons butter in a small skillet over medium-low heat. Add the shallot and garlic and cook until soft, about 3 minutes. Season lightly with salt and pepper. Then carefully add the cognac (use caution—it may ignite). Cook until the liquid in the skillet has evaporated, about 6 minutes. Remove from the heat and set aside.

2. Place a china cap or other coarse strainer over a bowl, and add the confit pork, allowing the oil to drain off. (It is okay to leave any fat still attached to the pork pieces.) Place the pork and any soft garlic pieces in a medium bowl. (Remove and discard the juniper berries, peppercorns, and bay leaves.) Stir the pork and garlic with a spoon or a flexible rubber spatula until it is completely broken down and shredded; the pork will break apart easily. Add the softened butter, reserved shallot mixture, parsley, the ¼ teaspoon salt, and the ½ teaspoon black pepper. Stir until well combined, and set aside. (If you decide to refrigerate the rillette before using it, carefully warm it in a pan before serving. It is best enjoyed at room temperature or slightly warmer.)

3. Put the watercress in a small bowl and season it lightly with salt and pepper. Add 1 tablespoon of the Fig Vinaigrette and toss lightly to combine.

4. To assemble: Toast the bread, and spread each slice with enough mustard to cover. Spread ⅓ cup of the pork rillette over the mustard on each slice of toast. Top with some of the watercress salad and the cornichons. Drizzle with some more Fig Vinaigrette. Halve the toasts and serve immediately.

## Confit Pork

About 1 quart

2 pounds boneless pork butt, rinsed and patted dry

1 tablespoon kosher salt

8 sprigs fresh thyme

6 cloves garlic, smashed

4 bay leaves

2 teaspoons fennel seeds

1 teaspoon black peppercorns

½ teaspoon dried juniper berries

1 to 1½ cups vegetable oil

1. Cut the pork into 3-inch cubes and place them in a medium bowl. Add the salt, thyme sprigs, garlic, bay leaves, fennel seeds, peppercorns, and juniper berries, and mix to combine. Transfer the pork and aromatics to a container, cover, and refrigerate overnight.

2. Preheat the oven to 300°F.

3. Remove the pork from the refrigerator, rinse off the salt, and pat dry. Add the pork and the aromatics to a shallow 6-cup baking dish, just large enough to hold it in a single layer. Add 1 cup of the vegetable oil, plus more if needed to just barely cover the pork. Cover the dish tightly with aluminum foil and set it on a rimmed baking sheet. Bake for 2½ to 3 hours, until the meat is fork-tender.

4. Remove the dish from the oven and allow the pork to cool in the fat for at least 1 hour before proceeding; or refrigerate, still immersed in its fat, for up to 1 week.

# CRAB LOUIE SANDWICH

6 sandwiches

This is a spin on the classic Crab Louie salad hailing from the West Coast. Typically the salad is made with Dungeness crabmeat, and if that's what's available, by all means use it. Here in Louisiana, though, we love our blue crabs. Either way, this sandwich is piled high with jumbo lump crabmeat. This is sheer indulgence and worth every bite.

1 cup mayonnaise, homemade (see page 309), or store-bought

¼ cup chili sauce

2 tablespoons chopped fresh chives

2 tablespoons chopped fresh parsley leaves

1 tablespoon freshly squeezed lemon juice

½ teaspoon finely grated lemon zest

½ teaspoon prepared horseradish

¼ teaspoon Worcestershire sauce

¼ teaspoon your favorite Louisiana red hot sauce

¼ teaspoon salt

¼ teaspoon freshly ground black pepper

1 pound jumbo lump crabmeat, cleaned of shells

6 slices brioche bread (see page 272), toasted

12 leaves Bibb lettuce

12 slices heirloom tomato

2 avocados, peeled, pitted, and thinly sliced

2 hard-boiled eggs, thinly sliced

½ cup sunflower sprouts or chervil sprigs, for garnish

1. In a medium mixing bowl, combine the mayonnaise, chili sauce, chives, parsley, lemon juice, lemon zest, horseradish, Worcestershire, and hot sauce. Season with the salt and pepper, and stir well. Remove ½ cup of the sauce and set it aside. Add the crabmeat to the remaining sauce and toss gently until well combined, taking care not to break up the crabmeat.

2. To assemble: Lay the toast on a cutting board and spread some of the reserved sauce over each slice. Top each with 2 lettuce leaves, 2 slices of tomato, 3 or 4 slices of avocado, and 3 slices of egg. Mound ½ cup of the crab salad on top. Divide the sunflower sprouts equally among the sandwiches, and serve.

# PAN-ROASTED SALMON WITH SHAVED FENNEL, OVEN-ROASTED TOMATOES, AND LEMONY RICOTTA SPREAD

8 sandwiches, 4 servings

There's nothing more delicious and healthful than wild salmon, which is what I recommend you use for this sandwich if at all possible. It seems that salmon goes well with just about everything—here the shaved fennel, roasted tomatoes, and lemony ricotta create a light, summery sandwich. Go ahead—serve it for dinner!

½ cup ricotta cheese

1 tablespoon finely grated lemon zest

¼ cup extra-virgin olive oil

1¼ + ⅛ teaspoons salt

¾ teaspoon freshly ground black pepper

1 medium bulb fennel

2 tablespoons freshly squeezed lemon juice

1½ pounds salmon fillets, skin and pin bones removed,
    cut into ¼-inch-thick slices

¼ cup instant flour, such as Wondra

8 slices sourdough sandwich bread

Easy Oven-Roasted Tomatoes (recipe follows)

½ cup Basil Spread (page 318)

1. In a small bowl, combine the ricotta, lemon zest, 1 tablespoon of the olive oil, ⅛ teaspoon of the salt, and ⅛ teaspoon of the pepper. Set aside.

2. Remove and discard the fennel stalks but reserve any fennel fronds. Using a mandoline or a very sharp knife, shave the fennel as thin as possible. Place the fennel in a small bowl, and toss it with the lemon juice, 1 tablespoon olive oil, ¼ teaspoon salt, and ⅛ teaspoon pepper. Set aside.

3. Heat a 12-inch sauté pan over medium-high heat. Add 1 tablespoon of the olive oil to the pan. Season the salmon with the remaining 1 teaspoon salt and ½ teaspoon pepper, and dip the slices in the flour, shaking to remove any excess. Place half of the salmon slices in the pan and sear for 1 minute; then turn them over to finish cooking on the second side, about 1 minute longer. Transfer the salmon to a paper-towel-lined plate. Repeat with the remaining 1 tablespoon olive oil and salmon.

4. Lightly toast the bread slices in a toaster or a warm oven.

5. To assemble: Spoon 1 tablespoon of the ricotta spread over each slice of toast. Divide the roasted tomato halves evenly over the ricotta spread, and spoon 1 teaspoon of the Basil Spread over the tomatoes. Lay 3 slices of the salmon onto each, and top with some of the shaved fennel. Garnish with the fennel fronds and drizzle with some of the remaining Basil Spread. Serve immediately.

Note: We love turning these into tiny sandwich bites, too, as shown in the photo on page 158. Simply cut the toast into small pieces and divide the ingredients accordingly. These small "sandwiches" make a wonderful hors d'oeuvre to serve with cocktails.

## Easy Oven-Roasted Tomatoes

1½ cups

2 pounds Roma or Campari tomatoes, cored and cut in half

¼ cup olive oil, plus more for storing if desired

2 tablespoons fresh thyme leaves

1 teaspoon sea salt

½ teaspoon freshly ground black pepper

1. Preheat the oven to 500°F. Line a baking sheet with aluminum foil.

2. In a medium mixing bowl, toss the tomatoes with the ¼ cup olive oil, thyme, sea salt, and pepper. Then transfer them to the baking sheet, cut side down. Roast the tomatoes for 5 minutes, or until the skin begins to shrink and come off the tomatoes. Carefully remove and discard the skins. Reduce the oven temperature to 250°F, and continue to roast the tomatoes until they are almost dry yet still slightly plump, about 2 hours.

3. To store, pack the tomatoes into clean jars, cover with olive oil, and refrigerate; or freeze them in plastic bags.

# PORCHETTA WITH DANDELION GREENS

6 to 8 sandwiches

This rich pork roast, stuffed with garlic and herbs, is a specialty of central Italy. Traditionally a whole pig is stuffed and slow-roasted over coals, producing the crispiest skin and tenderest, most succulent meat. It's considered a celebratory dish in Italy, and let me tell you, when you eat this, there will be a lot to celebrate! *Tip:* You'll need to start this recipe a day ahead, since the pork marinates overnight in the fridge.

¾ cup olive oil

¼ cup chopped fresh sage leaves

¼ cup chopped fresh fennel fronds

1 tablespoon chopped fresh thyme leaves

1 tablespoon chopped fresh rosemary leaves

1 tablespoon chopped fresh oregano leaves

1 tablespoon minced shallot

7 cloves garlic: 5 minced, 2 sliced

1 teaspoon finely grated orange zest

1 teaspoon finely grated lemon zest

½ teaspoon fennel seeds

¼ teaspoon coriander seeds

¼ cup dry white wine

2 tablespoons plus ¼ teaspoon sea salt

1 tablespoon freshly ground black pepper

6 pounds boneless pork shoulder,

    preferably with the skin still attached,

    or boneless pork butt with the fat cap attached

    (ask your butcher to butterfly to an even 1-inch thickness)

1 bunch fresh dandelion greens

6 to 8 thick slices olive fougasse or soft Italian bread, lightly toasted

1. In the bowl of a blender or food processor, combine ½ cup of the olive oil with the sage, fennel fronds, thyme, rosemary, oregano, shallot, minced garlic, orange and lemon zest, fennel seeds, coriander seeds, white wine, 1½ teaspoons of the salt, and 1 teaspoon of the pepper. Process for 45 seconds, or until the ingredients are well combined.

2. Lay the pork, skin side or fatty side down, on a cutting board, and spread the herb-oil mixture all over it. Roll the pork into a tight cylinder, and then tie it in several places with butcher's twine. Place the pork on a baking sheet, seam side down. Cover and refrigerate overnight.

3. Remove the pork from the refrigerator and allow it to sit at room temperature for up to 1 hour.

4. Preheat the oven to 500°F.

5. Rub the outside of the pork with 2 tablespoons olive oil, and then season the pork with 4½ teaspoons salt and the remaining 2 teaspoons pepper. Place the pork in a medium roasting pan—the pan should be just slightly larger than the roast. Place the pan in the oven and immediately reduce the temperature to 250°F. Roast the pork, uncovered, until it registers an internal temperature of 165°F on an instant-read thermometer, 4½ hours. If the skin does not seem crisp at the end of 4½ hours, raise the heat to 450°F and roast for 15 to 30 minutes, until a crispy crust is formed.

6. Remove the pork from the oven and let it rest for at least 20 minutes. When ready to serve, slice the meat crosswise into 1-inch-thick pieces.

7. Heat the remaining 2 tablespoons olive oil in a large sauté pan over medium-high heat. Add the sliced garlic and cook for 30 seconds, or just until the garlic is fragrant. Add the dandelion greens, a handful at a time, and cook until just wilted. Season with the remaining ¼ teaspoon salt.

8. Lay a slice of pork on each slice of toast, drizzle with some of the pan juices, and then top with a mound of dandelion greens. Serve immediately.

Note: The pork roast will yield more meat than is needed for the sandwiches, but it makes great leftovers. Store it in a resealable container in the refrigerator for 3 to 5 days.

# NEW ORLEANS SHRIMP MELT

8 sandwiches, 4 servings

New Orleanians are always looking for ways to use the abundance of fresh Gulf shrimp. Shrimp salad is not only a classic but a staple down here. What could make a shrimp salad better? How about melting cheese over the top and making a shrimp melt? Now that's what I'm talking about.

4 quarts water

1 tablespoon liquid crab boil, preferably Zatarain's

2 lemons, cut in half

2 bay leaves

Salt

2 pounds medium shrimp (16–20 count per pound),
    peeled and deveined

8 slices brioche (see page 272) or challah bread

6 tablespoons (¾ stick) unsalted butter,
    at room temperature

½ cup mayonnaise, homemade (see page 309),
    or store-bought

¼ cup minced red onion

2 tablespoons chopped fresh flat-leaf parsley leaves

1 tablespoon chopped fresh chives

1 tablespoon freshly squeezed lemon juice

1 teaspoon Dijon mustard

¼ teaspoon Crystal or your favorite Louisiana red hot sauce

Freshly ground black pepper, for seasoning

1½ cups shredded Gruyère cheese

1. In a 6-quart saucepan set over high heat, combine the water with 2 teaspoons of the crab boil, the lemons, the bay leaves, and a generous amount of salt (enough to make it taste almost like seawater), and bring to a boil.

2. Prepare an ice bath, and add the remaining 1 teaspoon crab boil to it along with enough salt to make the water taste like the sea.

3. Add the shrimp to the boiling water and cook for 2 minutes. Immediately transfer the shrimp to the ice bath and allow them to cool. As soon as the shrimp are cool enough to handle, chop them into bite-size pieces.

4. Position a rack 6 to 8 inches from the broiler element and preheat the broiler.

5. Spread one side of each slice of bread with the butter, and set on a baking sheet, buttered side up. Broil until toasted, 1 to 2 minutes. Then remove from the oven and set aside. Reduce the oven temperature to 400°F and move the rack to the upper third of the oven, if necessary.

6. In a large bowl, mix together the mayonnaise, red onion, parsley, chives, lemon juice, mustard, and hot sauce. Season with salt and pepper. Fold in the chopped shrimp.

7. Top the brioche slices with the shrimp salad, and sprinkle with the Gruyère. Bake in the upper third of the oven until the cheese is melted, about 7 minutes. Serve immediately.

# FRENCH BREAD PIZZA SANDWICHES WITH HOT ITALIAN SAUSAGE

4 sandwiches, 4 servings

Hey, guys, it doesn't get much easier than this. Here we top fresh garlic bread with tomato sauce, cheese, and sausage. Work fast, because your guests will hardly be able to wait for you to bake it with the toppings—the smell from the baking bread alone is enough to make 'em crazy. And go ahead, the buck doesn't stop here: Use your favorite toppings.

8 tablespoons (1 stick) unsalted butter

2 teaspoons minced garlic

¼ teaspoon salt

1 teaspoon freshly squeezed lemon juice

1 tablespoon minced fresh parsley leaves

1 loaf French or Italian bread, about 22 inches long

1 tablespoon olive oil

1½ pounds hot Italian sausage,
    casings removed and meat crumbled

2 cups Quick Tomato Sauce (page 183) or
    other marinara sauce

8 ounces mozzarella cheese, grated

8 ounces Fontina cheese, grated

2 tablespoons chopped fresh thyme leaves

½ teaspoon crushed red pepper

¼ cup finely grated Parmigiano-Reggiano cheese

Extra-virgin olive oil, for drizzling (optional)

1. Preheat the oven to 350°F. Line a baking sheet with aluminum foil or parchment paper for easier cleanup.

2. Melt the butter in a small pan, and combine it with the garlic, salt, lemon juice, and parsley.

3. Halve the bread lengthwise and cut each half in half crosswise. Using your fingers, gently scoop out and discard some of the soft inner part of the thickest portion of the bread, leaving a 1-inch-thick shell. Brush the inside of the bread with the garlic butter. Place the sections, cut side up, on the prepared baking sheet, and bake in the oven until golden, aromatic, and lightly toasted, about 6 minutes. Remove the bread from the oven (leave it on the baking sheet) and raise the oven temperature to 400°F.

4. Heat the olive oil in a medium skillet over medium heat. Add the sausage and cook, stirring as needed, until it is browned and the fat is rendered, about 8 minutes. Using a slotted spoon, transfer the sausage to a paper-towel-lined plate, and set aside.

5. Spoon the tomato sauce evenly over the pieces of bread. Divide the mozzarella and Fontina evenly over the sauce. Top with the sausage, and then garnish with the thyme, crushed red pepper, and Parmesan. Bake for 8 minutes, or until hot and bubbly. Serve immediately, drizzled with extra-virgin olive oil if desired.

# SANDWICH CAPRESE

4 servings

This delectable sandwich relies on the very best of just a few simple ingredients. Make this only when you have the finest tomatoes, the most prized mozzarella, and your special extra-virgin olive oil on hand—because in this recipe, the whole is truly only as good as its parts.

1 loaf ciabatta, sliced crosswise into 1-inch-thick slices (at least 8 slices)

1 tablespoon chopped garlic

¼ cup olive oil

Salt and freshly ground black pepper, for seasoning

2 tablespoons chopped fresh basil leaves, plus ½ cup basil chiffonade

8 ounces mozzarella di bufala, cut into ¼-inch-thick slices

2 pounds ripe heirloom tomatoes, cut into ½-inch-thick slices

Very good-quality extra-virgin olive oil, for drizzling

1. Preheat the oven to 400°F.

2. Arrange the slices of bread on a baking sheet. Combine the chopped garlic with 2 tablespoons of the olive oil, and brush over both sides of the bread. Lightly season them with salt and pepper, and bake for 10 minutes. Carefully turn the slices over and toast for 2 minutes longer. Remove from the oven. Combine the chopped basil with the remaining 2 tablespoons olive oil, and brush over the warm toast.

3. Shingle the mozzarella evenly over the toast. Shingle the tomato slices over the mozzarella. Lightly season the tomatoes with salt and pepper, top with the basil chiffonade, and drizzle with extra-virgin olive oil. Serve immediately.

# SMASHED CHICKPEAS ON NAAN WITH CILANTRO-MINT CHUTNEY

4 sandwiches

This simple open-face sandwich filled with Indian flavors is better than anything you'll get at a restaurant. Don't fret if you don't have all the ingredients—for example, you can substitute raw sugar or light brown sugar for the palm sugar, or clarified butter for the ghee if necessary.

2 tablespoons ghee or clarified butter

1 tablespoon yellow mustard seeds

½ cup minced red onion

2 teaspoons minced garlic

1 teaspoon minced fresh ginger

½ teaspoon crushed red pepper

Two 15-ounce cans chickpeas, drained (about 4 cups)

2 tomatoes, chopped

1 red bell pepper, diced

1 teaspoon ground turmeric

1 teaspoon ground cumin

½ teaspoon ground cardamom

½ teaspoon ground coriander

½ teaspoon sea salt

¼ cup chopped fresh cilantro leaves

4 pieces naan bread, warmed

1 recipe Cilantro-Mint Chutney (page 340)

1 recipe Raita (page 321)

1. Melt the ghee in a large sauté pan over medium-high heat. Add the yellow mustard seeds and cook until the seeds begin to pop, 3 to 4 minutes. Add the red onion, garlic, ginger, and crushed red pepper, and cook until the onion is soft, about 4 minutes. Add the chickpeas, tomatoes, bell pepper, turmeric, cumin, cardamom, coriander, and salt. Cook for 15 to 20 minutes, until the flavors come together. Using a potato masher, gently mash about half of the chickpeas. Add the cilantro and stir to combine.

2. Spoon the chickpeas onto the warmed naan bread. Garnish with the Cilantro-Mint Chutney and the Raita. Serve immediately.

# QUADRELLO DI BUFALA WITH PAN-CRISPED PROSCIUTTO, HONEYED FIGS, AND FRISÉE

8 sandwiches, 4 servings

Quadrello di Bufala is essentially a Taleggio cheese made with buffalo milk. It is outrageously good if you like a rich, creamy, washed-rind cheese that just melts in your mouth. Pan-frying the prosciutto makes it a crispy, delicious alternative to bacon, and the honeyed figs round this whole sandwich out with just a hint of something sweet.

8 slices rustic country bread or whole-wheat sourdough bread

5 tablespoons extra-virgin olive oil

¼ teaspoon sea salt

¼ teaspoon freshly ground black pepper

12 ounces Quadrello di Bufala or Taleggio cheese, sliced

2 ounces sliced prosciutto di Parma

¼ cup raw unfiltered honey

4 fresh black Mission figs, stemmed and sliced into ¼-inch-thick rounds

2 sprigs fresh thyme

1 tablespoon fig-infused vinegar

1 cup rinsed, spun dry, and chopped frisée lettuce (1-inch pieces)

½ cup julienned firm-ripe pear

1. Position an oven rack 6 to 8 inches from the broiler unit, and preheat the broiler.

2. Brush one side of the slices of bread with 2 tablespoons of the olive oil, and season with the salt and pepper. Divide the cheese slices evenly among the bread. Place the cheese-topped bread on a baking sheet and set aside.

3. Heat a medium sauté pan over medium heat, and add 2 tablespoons of the olive oil. Add 2 slices of the prosciutto to the pan and cook for 2 minutes per side, or until it is very crispy. Transfer the prosciutto to a paper-towel-lined plate and repeat with the remaining prosciutto.

4. Add the honey to the same sauté pan and heat it over medium heat until it begins to bubble, about 30 seconds. Add the figs and the thyme sprigs, and cook for 2 minutes, until warmed through. Set aside.

5. Place the baking sheet under the broiler, and toast the bread for 4 to 5 minutes, until the cheese is melted.

6. In a small mixing bowl, combine the fig vinegar with the remaining 1 tablespoon olive oil. Add the frisée and the pear, and toss to coat.

7. Top each cheese toast with 1 slice of the crisped prosciutto. Then spoon several slices of the honeyed figs over the prosciutto. Garnish each slice with the frisée and pear mixture, and serve immediately.

Tunisian Street Sandwich,
see pages 203–206

# ALL WRAPPED UP

# FALAFEL WITH CUCUMBER, ONION, AND TOMATO SALAD

6 servings

Falafel masters, watch out for the home cook who makes this one! The flavor is a slam dunk and the method is just too easy. You don't have to go out for really good falafel anymore—and you definitely won't go back to the mix!

1 cup dried chickpeas,
    soaked in 4 cups of water for 24 hours
1 cup dried split fava beans,
    soaked in 4 cups of water for 24 hours
1 cup chopped onion
¼ cup roughly chopped fresh parsley leaves
¼ cup roughly chopped fresh cilantro leaves
4 cloves garlic
1 tablespoon ground cumin
2 teaspoons salt
1 teaspoon ground coriander
¼ teaspoon crushed red pepper
½ teaspoon baking soda
3 tablespoons freshly squeezed lemon juice
Vegetable oil, for frying
6 pita breads (see page 290)
Cucumber, Onion, and Tomato Salad (recipe follows)
Tahini Sauce (page 320), for serving
Hot sauce or Classic Red Harissa (page 322), for serving (optional)

1. Drain and rinse the chickpeas and fava beans, and put them in the bowl of a food processor. Add the onion, parsley, cilantro, garlic, cumin, salt, coriander, crushed red pepper, baking soda, and lemon juice. Process, scraping down the sides of the bowl with a rubber spatula as necessary, until the mixture is uniform and can hold a shape when gently pressed together with your fingers. Transfer the mixture to a bowl, cover, and set aside for 30 minutes.

2. Using a 2-tablespoon scoop, portion out the fava-chickpea mixture. Then gently form the scoops into patties. Set them aside on a plate.

3. Fill a 12- to 14-inch sauté pan with vegetable oil to a depth of 1½ inches, and heat it to 350°F. Using a metal spatula and working in batches, making sure not to crowd the pan, gently lower the falafel patties into the hot oil and fry until they are crisp and brown on one side, 1½ to 2 minutes. Flip the patties over and cook until crisp and brown on the other side, 1½ to 2 minutes longer. Transfer the patties to a paper-towel-lined plate and repeat with the remaining mixture.

4. To assemble: Cut each pita bread to form a pocket, and fill it with some Cucumber, Onion, and Tomato Salad, falafel patties, Tahini Sauce, and hot sauce if desired. (Alternatively, you can wrap the ingredients in the pita, or place the components on a platter and allow guests to serve themselves.)

## Cucumber, Onion, and Tomato Salad

6 to 8 cups

1 small head romaine lettuce, shredded or finely chopped

1 sweet yellow onion, or 8 green onions, finely chopped

2 medium cucumbers, peeled, seeded, and cut into small dice

2 to 3 ripe tomatoes, finely diced

3 tablespoons chopped fresh parsley leaves

2 tablespoons chopped fresh mint leaves

1 tablespoon chopped fresh dill

¼ cup plus 2 tablespoons fresh lemon juice

1 small clove garlic, finely minced

9 tablespoons extra-virgin olive oil

Salt and freshly ground black pepper, for seasoning

1. Combine the lettuce, onion, cucumbers, tomatoes, parsley, mint, and dill in a salad bowl and toss to combine thoroughly.

2. In a separate bowl, whisk together the lemon juice, garlic, and olive oil, and season to taste with salt and pepper. Drizzle over the salad, toss well to combine, and serve immediately.

# BEEF SHAWARMA
# WITH TZATZIKI SAUCE

4 to 6 sandwiches

The shawarma, also known as the gyro, is a traditional Middle Eastern sandwich made generally with lamb, beef, and sometimes chicken that has been marinated and grilled or barbecued. The keys to this sandwich are twofold: the marinade for the meat and the tzatziki sauce served with it.

½ cup plain Greek-style yogurt

¼ cup red wine vinegar

¼ cup plus 2 tablespoons olive oil

1 tablespoon fresh lemon juice

2 cloves garlic, smashed

2 teaspoons freshly ground black pepper

1 teaspoon ground cumin

1 teaspoon ground cinnamon

1 teaspoon ground allspice

½ teaspoon ground cloves

½ teaspoon ground cardamom

2 pounds boneless beef sirloin, thinly sliced

4 to 6 large pita breads

2 teaspoons salt

1 cup thinly sliced red onion

2 tomatoes, chopped

4 cups chopped lettuce leaves

2 tablespoons chopped fresh parsley leaves

Tzatziki Sauce (page 321), for serving

Ground sumac, for garnish (optional)

Classic Red Harissa (page 322), for serving (optional)

1. In a medium mixing bowl, combine the yogurt, vinegar, ¼ cup olive oil, lemon juice, garlic, 1 teaspoon of the black pepper, the cumin, cinnamon, allspice, cloves, and cardamom, and mix well. Add the beef and mix thoroughly. Cover and refrigerate for at least 8 hours and up to overnight.

2. Preheat the oven to 200°F.

3. Wrap the pita breads in aluminum foil and place in the oven to warm.

4. Remove the beef from the marinade, and discard the marinade. Season the meat with the salt and the remaining 1 teaspoon pepper. Heat a large sauté pan over medium-high heat. Add 1 tablespoon olive oil to the pan and when it is hot, add half of the beef. Cook for 2 to 3 minutes, turning the slices over midway, until seared on both sides. Remove from the pan and repeat with the remaining 1 tablespoon olive oil and beef. Transfer the beef to a platter and keep it warm in the oven while making the sandwiches.

5. Arrange the warmed pita breads on a work surface, and scatter the onion, tomatoes, lettuce, parsley, and beef on the lower half of the breads. Drizzle with the Tzatziki Sauce, and sprinkle with sumac if desired. Roll up the pita breads and wrap the sandwiches in sheets of aluminum foil. Serve with extra Tzatziki Sauce and harissa if desired.

# SOPRESSATA AND GENOA SALAMI CALZONES

4 calzones

I love this calzone with a variety of salumi, but this is a recipe where you can safely go in many directions. Change up the cheese, use roasted red peppers or sautéed mushrooms instead of the meat, add Roasted Garlic (page 79) . . . I could go on and on. And you don't have to eat them right out of the oven, either—they travel well, so pack your picnic basket!

1 recipe Semolina Pizza Dough (page 298)

1 cup Quick Tomato Sauce for Calzones (recipe follows)
    or your favorite jarred pizza/pasta sauce

1 cup chopped fresh basil leaves

8 ounces mixed sopressata, hot sopressata, Genoa salami,
    and/or pepperoni, chopped

1 cup ricotta cheese, drained

8 ounces smoked mozzarella cheese, cut into ½-inch cubes

¼ cup finely grated Parmigiano-Reggiano cheese

½ teaspoon crushed red pepper

Flour or cornmeal, for dusting the pizza peel

1. Place a pizza stone in the bottom third of the oven and preheat the oven to 500°F. (Alternatively, place an upside-down rimmed baking sheet on the rack in your oven.)

2. Halve one of the pieces of dough and roll it out on a lightly floured work surface to form two 8-inch rounds. Spread ¼ cup of the tomato sauce over the bottom half of each round, leaving a 1-inch border. Sprinkle ¼ cup of the basil and one-quarter of the cured meats evenly over each portion of sauce. Sprinkle one-quarter of the

ricotta, mozzarella, Parmesan, and crushed red pepper over each portion of meat. Gently fold the top half of the dough over the filling, rolling and pressing the edges together with your fingertips to seal them, and crimping as you go along. Make 2 more calzones with the remaining ingredients.

3. Depending on the size of your oven, you may be able to bake only 2 calzones at a time. Cut several small slits in the top of each calzone to allow air to escape while baking, and transfer the calzones to a pizza peel that has been lightly dusted with flour or cornmeal (to facilitate moving the dough). Tilt the pizza peel to slide the calzones onto the preheated baking stone. Bake for 16 minutes, or until the top is golden brown and the dough is cooked through. Remove the calzones from the oven with the pizza peel or a spatula, and serve immediately or at room temperature.

## Quick Tomato Sauce for Calzones

1³/₄ cups

1 tablespoon olive oil

1 onion, chopped

3 cloves garlic, chopped

One 28-ounce can whole peeled tomatoes, drained and pureed

1 sprig fresh thyme

½ teaspoon salt

½ teaspoon freshly ground black pepper

1 tablespoon extra-virgin olive oil

Heat the olive oil in a small saucepan over medium heat. Add the onion and garlic, and cook for 3 minutes, until soft. Add the tomatoes, thyme sprig, salt, and pepper, and simmer for 20 minutes. Remove from the heat. Stir in the extra-virgin olive oil, discard the thyme sprig, and set aside until ready to use.

# FIVE-SPICE DUCK WITH HOISIN AND MANDARIN PANCAKES

16 wraps, 4 servings

How can one succulent roasted duck feed four people? Put it inside Chinese pancakes, of course! Throw in a little hoisin, green onion, and cucumber along the way—and it's a wrap.

One 5-pound duck, innards and excess fat around the neck
    removed and discarded, rinsed and patted dry inside and out
3 tablespoons minced green onion tops,
    plus 1 cup julienned green onion bottoms (from about 2 bunches)
2 tablespoons minced fresh ginger
1 tablespoon minced garlic
2 teaspoons finely grated orange zest
2½ teaspoons Chinese five-spice powder
1½ teaspoons salt
3 tablespoons soy sauce
½ cup freshly squeezed orange juice
2 tablespoons honey
1 teaspoon black bean garlic sauce or fermented black beans
Mandarin Pancakes (recipe follows)
⅓ cup hoisin sauce
1 cup peeled, seeded, and julienned cucumber, lightly salted

1. Place the duck on a rack set over a rimmed baking sheet. Refrigerate the duck, uncovered, allowing it to air-dry, for at least 2 hours and up to overnight.

2. In a small bowl, combine the green onion tops with the ginger, garlic, orange zest, 1 teaspoon of the five-spice powder, ½ teaspoon of the salt, and 2 tablespoons of the soy sauce. Set aside.

3. Preheat the oven to 350°F.

4. Remove the duck from the refrigerator and pat the inside dry once more. Using a sharp knife, score the skin all over in a crosshatch pattern, being careful not to cut deep enough to expose the flesh. Rub the inside of the duck with the green onion mixture, and then tie the legs together with kitchen twine. Fold the wing tips, if still attached, behind the duck. Season the outside of the duck with the remaining 1 teaspoon salt and the remaining 1½ teaspoons five-spice powder.

5. Return the duck to the rack set over the baking sheet, place it in the oven, and roast for 30 minutes.

6. While the duck is roasting, combine the orange juice, honey, black bean garlic sauce, and remaining 1 tablespoon soy sauce in a small saucepan. Bring it to a boil over medium heat. Then reduce the heat to a simmer and cook until the liquid has reduced enough to coat the back of a spoon, about 8 minutes. Remove the pan from the heat and set it aside.

7. Carefully remove the duck from the oven and gently prick the skin all over with a sharp knife to release some of the hot fat. Turn the duck over, breast side down, on the rack and roast for 30 minutes. Remove the duck from the oven, turn it breast side up on the rack, prick the skin again, and roast for another 30 minutes.

8. Remove the duck from the oven and prick it a final time (do not turn it). Raise the oven temperature to 400°F. Brush the duck all over with the orange-soy glaze. Roast for a final 10 minutes. Then set it aside until cool enough to handle. While the duck is resting, make the Mandarin Pancakes.

9. When the duck is cool enough to handle, transfer the drippings from the baking sheet to a small bowl. Pour off and discard the fat from the top, or use a spoon to separate the fat from the juices. Using kitchen shears, cut along both sides of the

duck's backbone and remove the bone. Then cut along the breastbone, dividing the duck in half. Using your hands, remove and discard the wishbone, rib bones, and thigh and leg bones. Set the duck on a cutting board and slice it thinly. Transfer the slices to a small platter, and pour the reserved juices over the meat to moisten it.

10. To assemble: Spread a teaspoon of hoisin sauce over a pancake. Line some of the cucumber and julienned green onion in the center, and then top with a tablespoon of the duck. Enclose the filling by rolling the pancake. Repeat with the rest of the wraps.

## Mandarin Pancakes

16 pancakes

These are the pancakes that are generally served with moo shu pork and Peking duck. They're easy and very fun to make. You roll two dough pieces together, cook them, then pull them apart. It's like magic.

1½ cups all-purpose flour, plus more for dusting

¼ teaspoon plus a pinch of salt

¾ cup boiling water

About 2 tablespoons toasted sesame oil, for brushing

1. In a small bowl, mix the flour and salt together. Add the boiling water and stir with a spoon to combine. Using your hands, continue to incorporate the water with the flour until a dough forms. Transfer the dough to a clean work surface and knead it about 10 times, until the dough is smooth, warm, and soft. Cover it with a clean kitchen towel or plastic wrap, and let it rest for 30 minutes.

2. Lightly dust your hands with flour, and roll the dough into a 16-inch-long cylinder. Cut the cylinder into 1-inch-thick pieces, and roll each piece into a small ball.

3. Slightly flatten 2 dough balls into disks. Brush the tops with sesame oil, and press the oiled sides together. Using a rolling pin, roll out to form a 5- to 6-inch round. (It's okay if the edges of the pancakes don't match up perfectly.) Repeat until you have 8 rolled-out pairs.

4. Heat a dry skillet over medium heat. Cook one of the sets of pancakes for about a minute or so, until both sides are lightly browned. Remove the set from the skillet, and when it is just cool enough to handle, gently pull the paired pancakes apart. Cover them with a damp cloth to keep them from drying out. Continue with the remaining pancakes. Serve immediately.

# THAI-STYLE GRILLED CURRIED CHICKEN WITH TAMARIND SAUCE

4 to 6 servings

I love Thai satays so much, and what's not to love? For a twist, the marinade here calls for Thai red curry paste, which gives the chicken a wonderful flavor. And instead of the typical peanut sauce, you gotta try this Tamarind Sauce.

2½ pounds boneless, skinless chicken breasts

½ cup unsweetened coconut milk

¼ cup freshly squeezed lime juice

¼ cup palm sugar or packed light brown sugar

2 tablespoons plus 2 teaspoons fish sauce

2 tablespoons Thai red curry paste (I recommend Mae Ploy brand)

½ cup chopped fresh cilantro stems and leaves,
    plus 1 cup whole fresh cilantro leaves

¼ cup finely chopped shallot

1 tablespoon minced garlic

Kosher salt, for seasoning

2 heads green-leaf lettuce, leaves separated, rinsed, and spun dry

1 large red bell pepper, finely julienned

1 cup fresh mint leaves

Tamarind Sauce (page 345)

Special equipment: sixteen to eighteen 12-inch bamboo skewers,
    soaked in water

1. Cut the chicken breasts across the grain into strips ½ inch thick and 3 to 4 inches in length. Transfer them to a gallon-size resealable plastic food storage bag.

2. Combine the coconut milk, lime juice, sugar, fish sauce, curry paste, chopped cilantro, shallot, and garlic in a food processor and process until smooth. Pour half of the marinade over the chicken and toss to coat well. Seal the bag, removing as much of the air as possible, and place it on a plate in the refrigerator. Reserve the remaining half of the marinade for basting. Marinate the chicken for 3 to 4 hours, turning the bag over midway.

3. Thread the chicken onto the skewers, discarding the used marinade. Season both sides of the skewered chicken with salt.

4. Preheat a grill or grill pan to high.

5. In batches, place the skewers on the grill and cook until hatch marks appear and the chicken becomes opaque on one side, 1 to 3 minutes. Turn the skewers over and baste with the reserved marinade. Continue to cook for another 1 to 3 minutes, or until the chicken is nearly cooked through. Turn over again and baste before removing from the grill.

6. To assemble each wrap, wrap a lettuce leaf around the chicken and slide the meat off the skewer. Add a few slices of bell pepper and some mint and cilantro leaves to the chicken. Drizzle some of the Tamarind Sauce over the chicken, wrap the leaf around the filling, and enjoy hot.

# CHOPPED SALAD WRAP WITH PAN-ROASTED CHICKEN, ROQUEFORT, AND BACON

6 wraps

Chopped salads were created to be eaten easily with only a fork. Tidy it up this way in a tortilla and you can even eat it without! It's chopped, dressed, and wrapped. These sandwiches are made extra delicious with the homemade ranch dressing spread and the creamiest blue cheese you can find.

1 pound boneless, skinless chicken breasts
   (or skip step 1 and use leftover cooked chicken, turkey, or ham)

1½ teaspoons Emeril's Original Essence or
   Creole Seasoning (page 9)

3 tablespoons olive oil or vegetable oil

½ teaspoon Dijon mustard

2 tablespoons red wine vinegar

2 tablespoons chopped fresh parsley leaves

2 tablespoons minced green onion

1 teaspoon minced garlic

½ cup plus 2 tablespoons sour cream

1 teaspoon salt

½ teaspoon freshly ground black pepper

1½ cups chopped iceberg lettuce

1½ cups chopped radicchio

½ cup chopped cucumber

½ cup grated carrot

½ cup halved cherry tomatoes

8 ounces applewood-smoked bacon,
    chopped and cooked until crisp

2 hard-boiled eggs, chopped

1 avocado, peeled, pitted, and chopped

4 ounces Roquefort, Gorgonzola dolce,
    or your favorite blue cheese

¼ teaspoon crushed red pepper

Six 10-inch flour tortillas


1. Preheat the oven to 400°F.

2. Season the chicken all over with the Essence. Heat 1 tablespoon of the oil in an
ovenproof skillet over high heat, add the chicken, and cook for 2 minutes per side.
Then transfer the skillet to the oven and cook for 8 minutes longer, until the chicken
is just cooked through and the thickest part registers 165°F on an instant-read
thermometer. Set the chicken aside to cool. When it is cool enough to handle, chop the
chicken and refrigerate it until ready to use.

3. Combine the mustard and vinegar in a small bowl. Whisk in the remaining 2
tablespoons oil. Set the vinaigrette aside.

4. In a medium bowl, combine the parsley, green onion, garlic, sour cream, ½ teaspoon
of the salt, and ¼ teaspoon of the pepper. Refrigerate until ready to use.

5. In a large bowl, combine the iceberg lettuce, radicchio, cucumber, carrot, tomatoes,
bacon, eggs, and avocado. Break up the cheese into small pieces and add them to the
bowl. Add the chopped chicken, and season with the remaining ½ teaspoon salt, the
remaining ¼ teaspoon black pepper, and the crushed red pepper. Using a large spoon,
gently combine all the ingredients. Give the reserved vinaigrette a quick whisk, add it
to the bowl, and toss to combine.

6. Heat a large skillet over medium-high heat. Add a tortilla and cook on both sides until lightly browned, about 1 minute. Remove the tortilla from the pan and repeat with the remaining tortillas.

7. To assemble: Spoon a generous tablespoon of the sour cream mixture in a line across the center of a warmed tortilla. Measure a generous cup of the salad, and spoon it in a line on top of the sour cream. Working from left to right (or if you prefer, right to left), fold one side of the tortilla over the mixture by about an inch, and hold it in place with your hand. With your other hand, roll the tortilla away from you, fitting it tightly around the mixture. Continue to roll the tortilla into a tight cylinder until the seam is on the bottom. Repeat with the remaining tortillas and filling, and serve immediately.

# FRESH TUNA AND BUTTER LETTUCE WRAPS WITH CRISPY TORTILLA STRIPS, MARINATED RED CABBAGE, AND SHAVED JALAPEÑO

4 large appetizer servings or 2 entrée servings

The lettuce leaves here take the place of traditional wraps, making this a lighter option—yet these are so full of flavor that it's a party on a lettuce leaf. Prepare the components ahead of time if you like, then just throw these together when you're ready to serve them.

2 tablespoons olive oil, plus more for frying

8 ounces sushi-grade yellowfin tuna fillet

1 teaspoon kosher salt, plus more for seasoning

¼ teaspoon freshly ground black pepper

3 corn tortillas, halved and then cut into ⅛-inch-wide strips

16 large leaves butter lettuce (from about 2 heads),
    rinsed and spun dry

¾ cup Marinated Red Cabbage (recipe follows),
    drained

Spicy chili garlic sauce, preferably Sriracha,
    for garnish

1 large jalapeño, thinly shaved crosswise
    using a mandoline or a very sharp knife

Bagna Cauda Drizzle (page 316), for serving

1. In a 12-inch sauté pan, heat the 2 tablespoons olive oil over high heat. Season the tuna on all sides with the 1 teaspoon kosher salt and the black pepper. Quickly sear the tuna on all sides, 10 to 15 seconds per side for rare. When it is cool enough to handle, slice the tuna into ¼-inch-thick slices (you should end up with about 16 slices). Set them aside.

2. Wipe the sauté pan clean with a paper towel. Add oil to a depth of ½ to 1 inch, and heat it over medium-high heat. When the oil is hot, cook the tortilla strips, in batches, until golden brown, 30 to 45 seconds. Using a slotted spoon, transfer them to a paper-towel-lined plate to drain. Immediately season each batch with a pinch of salt. Set aside.

3. Divide the lettuce leaves into 4 portions, and arrange them on four appetizer plates. Place a small amount of the crispy tortilla strips in the center of each leaf and top with 1 to 2 tablespoons of the Marinated Red Cabbage. Lay a slice of tuna over the cabbage, sprinkle with a pinch of salt, and place a dot of chili garlic sauce on the tuna. Follow with the jalapeño slices and drizzle with the Bagna Cauda Drizzle, to taste. Serve immediately.

## Marinated Red Cabbage

About 3 cups

This is delicious enough to serve as a side—it goes great with pork, too. If you make it ahead of time, the flavor only gets better, and on a busy day, all you have to do is pull it out of the fridge and enjoy.

8 ounces red cabbage, thinly sliced
1½ teaspoons kosher salt
½ cup freshly squeezed orange juice

½ cup white wine vinegar

¼ cup sugar

1. Place the cabbage in a nonreactive bowl, sprinkle the kosher salt over it, and toss to combine. Let it sit for about 1 hour at room temperature, tossing it occasionally.

2. Place the orange juice, vinegar, and sugar in a small saucepan and bring to a boil over medium-high heat. Cook until the liquid has reduced to ½ cup, about 6 minutes. Remove from the heat and set aside to cool.

3. Rinse and drain the cabbage, and then squeeze out as much moisture as possible. Return it to the bowl. When the orange juice mixture is cool, pour it over the cabbage and toss to combine. Let it sit, for at least 1 hour at room temperature or up to overnight in the refrigerator, before serving.

# BARBACOA TACOS

Enough meat for approximately 20 tacos, about 6 servings

Barbacoa is, in the simplest terms, the original barbecue. In modern-day Mexico it can take on many forms, though traditionally it refers to meat wrapped in leaves and cooked over hot coals in a pit. The result: moist, tender meat that is then shredded or pulled apart and eaten with simple, intensely flavored sauces and soft tortillas. Today many cooks achieve similar results by braising or steaming, and that's what I've done here.

### Beef

One boneless 3-pound chuck roast

6 cloves garlic, halved lengthwise

2 teaspoons kosher salt

½ teaspoon freshly ground black pepper

2 tablespoons vegetable oil

1 medium onion, finely chopped

2 sprigs fresh thyme

2 bay leaves

2 teaspoons ground cumin

2 teaspoons dried Mexican oregano, crumbled between your fingers

⅛ teaspoon ground cloves

⅛ teaspoon ground allspice

1 medium tomato, cored and finely chopped

2 chipotle chiles in adobo, finely chopped (about 2 tablespoons)

3 tablespoons cider vinegar

1½ cups beef stock or packaged low-sodium beef broth

## Tacos

20 small corn or flour tortillas, warmed according to package directions

2 avocados, peeled, seeded, and cut into thin lengthwise slices

Mexican crema or sour cream, for serving (optional)

Red Onion and Tomato Salsa Fresca (page 328) or your favorite salsa, for serving

1. To make the barbacoa: Remove the chuck roast from the refrigerator and allow it to sit out at room temperature for at least 30 minutes and up to 1 hour.

2. Preheat the oven to 325°F.

3. Using the tip of a sharp paring knife, make 12 evenly spaced slits on all sides of the roast, and insert half a garlic clove deep into each slit. Season the roast on both sides with the salt and black pepper.

4. Heat a large Dutch oven over high heat and add the oil. When the oil is hot, add the roast and cook until nicely browned on one side, 4 to 6 minutes. Turn the roast over and continue cooking until browned on the second side, 4 to 6 minutes longer. While the roast is browning on the second side, add the onion, thyme sprigs, bay leaves, cumin, oregano, cloves, and allspice around the meat in the pot and cook, stirring occasionally. The vegetables should be soft by the time the roast is done browning.

5. Add the tomato and cook until it releases its juices, 1 to 2 minutes. Add the chipotle chiles, cider vinegar, and beef stock, and bring to a simmer. Cover the pot and transfer it to the oven. Braise, turning the roast once every hour, until the meat is fork-tender and falling apart, 3 to 3½ hours.

6. Remove the pot from the oven and discard the bay leaves and thyme sprigs. Using two forks, shred the meat. Stir the shredded meat gently to combine it with the pan juices. Then cover to keep it warm until ready to serve.

7. To assemble the tacos: Spoon about ¼ cup of the shredded meat down the center of a warmed tortilla, and top with 2 thin slices of avocado. Drizzle with some of the crema, and spoon a bit of salsa on top. Repeat with the remaining tacos.

# BIG EMPANADAS

6 servings

Empanadas, sometimes known as meat pies, are enjoyed in many places—from Spain and Portugal to Indonesia and throughout Africa and Latin America. Even in other parts of the world you'll find deliciously filled savory pastries. Whether baked or fried, these babies are always a treat.

2 pounds Idaho potatoes, peeled and cut into
   ¼-inch dice (about 4 cups)

1¼ teaspoons salt, plus more for seasoning

1 tablespoon vegetable oil, plus more if needed

2 pounds ground beef

2 onions, chopped (about 4 cups)

2 red or green bell peppers, or a combination,
   chopped (about 2 cups)

¼ cup chopped fresh cilantro stems,
   plus 2 teaspoons chopped leaves

1 tablespoon minced garlic

¼ cup Madeira

1 cup beef stock or packaged
   low-sodium beef broth

1 tablespoon tomato paste

1 bay leaf

1 teaspoon paprika

¼ teaspoon ground cinnamon

¼ teaspoon crushed red pepper

¼ cup plus 2 tablespoons chopped pimento-stuffed

    Spanish olives (optional)

¼ cup chopped golden raisins or dried currants (optional)

Empanada Dough (recipe follows)

All-purpose flour, for dusting

1. Place the potatoes in a pot, cover with cold water, season with salt to taste, and bring to a boil. Cook the potatoes until just tender, 3 to 4 minutes. Drain the potatoes and set aside.

2. Heat 1 tablespoon of the oil in a large skillet over medium heat. Add the beef and cook until browned, about 5 minutes. Add the onions, bell peppers, cilantro stems, garlic, and 1 teaspoon of the salt. Cook until the vegetables are soft, about 5 minutes. Add the Madeira, beef stock, tomato paste, bay leaf, paprika, cinnamon, and crushed red pepper. Simmer for about 30 minutes, or until the flavors have mingled and most of the liquid has evaporated. Stir in the chopped cilantro leaves. Using a large slotted spoon, transfer the beef and vegetables to a large bowl.

3. Remove and discard all but 2 tablespoons of the fat from the skillet (if no fat remains, add 2 tablespoons vegetable oil to the skillet) and return the skillet to medium heat. When it is hot, add the potatoes and sauté until lightly browned on all sides, about 4 minutes. Season the potatoes with the remaining ¼ teaspoon salt, and transfer them to the bowl containing the beef. Add the olives and raisins, if using, and stir to combine. Set aside, or cover and refrigerate for up to 1 week.

4. Preheat the oven to 400°F.

5. Remove the empanada dough from the refrigerator and divide it into 6 portions (about 5 ounces each). Lightly dust a work surface and rolling pin with flour, and roll one of the portions into an 8-inch round. Pack a 1-cup measure with the meat filling, and place the filling in the center of the round. Stretch and fold the dough over the filling, and press the edges together to seal. Starting from one end of the empanada, twist the edge by folding it inward and crimping it, steadily moving along the side,

until you have "roped" the edge decoratively from one end to the other. Transfer the empanada to an ungreased cookie sheet. Repeat with the remaining dough and filling. Bake for 20 minutes, or until golden. Serve hot or at room temperature.

## Empanada Dough

Enough dough for 6 large empanadas

1 cup water

¾ cup solid vegetable shortening

2 tablespoons butter

3 cups all-purpose flour, plus more for dusting

2 teaspoons salt

2 egg yolks

1 teaspoon distilled white vinegar

1. Combine the water, shortening, and butter in a small saucepan and heat until melted. Set aside.

2. In a medium bowl, combine the flour and the salt. In a small bowl, whisk together the egg yolks and vinegar.

3. Make a well in the middle of the flour and whisk in about a cup of the melted shortening mixture to make a wet paste. Add the yolk mixture while continuing to add the warm liquid, about ½ cup at a time, whisking to incorporate the flour until all the liquid has been used. Transfer the dough to a work surface that has been lightly dusted with flour. Knead it several times with lightly floured hands until you have a wet, oily dough. Wrap the dough in plastic wrap and refrigerate it for at least 2 hours or up to overnight before using.

# TUNISIAN STREET SANDWICH

*4 turnovers*

This surprisingly delicious crisp and savory fried turnover gets its crackle from simple store-bought spring roll wrappers. Inside the crispy goodness is an intensely flavored tuna filling, a schmear of a delightful homemade harissa, and one perfectly cooked over-easy egg. Should you desire a firmer egg yolk, simply cook your turnover a few seconds longer—ten to twenty seconds more should do the trick.

One 6-ounce can albacore tuna in spring water, drained and crumbled

1 tablespoon roughly chopped fresh parsley leaves

1 tablespoon roughly chopped fresh cilantro leaves

3 tablespoons extra-virgin olive oil

3 teaspoons minced green onion

2 teaspoons minced preserved lemon rind (see Note)

2 canned anchovy fillets, mashed to a paste (a generous ½ teaspoon)

¼ teaspoon kosher salt

⅛ teaspoon freshly ground black pepper

Vegetable or peanut oil, for frying

Four 8-inch square spring roll wrappers,
   defrosted according to the package directions

1 egg, lightly whisked, plus 4 whole eggs

5 teaspoons harissa, homemade (see page 322), or
   store-bought, or to taste, plus more for serving

1. Place the tuna, parsley, and cilantro in a small bowl. In a separate small bowl, whisk together the extra-virgin olive oil, green onion, preserved lemon, anchovy,

salt, and pepper. Add the oil mixture to the tuna, and using the tines of a fork, mash until the mixture is thoroughly combined and the tuna is in small flakes.

2. Fill a heavy pan, such as a deep cast-iron skillet, with vegetable oil to a depth of 1 inch. Heat it over medium-high heat until the oil is hot but not smoking, between 350° and 375°F.

3. While the oil is heating, place 2 of the spring roll wrappers on a clean work surface (keep the remaining wrappers covered with a damp towel to prevent them from drying out). Position the wrappers so that one of the points is closest to you. Using your fingers, spread some of the lightly whisked egg along all the edges of the wrappers (this will help to form a seal when you press the edges together). Place one-quarter of the tuna mixture on the bottom half of each of the wrappers, and use a spoon or your fingers to form a shallow well in the mound of tuna. On the upper half of the wrappers, spread a heaping teaspoon of the harissa, reaching to within 1 inch of the edges.

4. Crack an egg into one of the tuna wells. Working quickly, fold the upper half of the wrapper (with the harissa) up and over the tuna and egg, and press the edges together to form a triangle-shaped packet. (See below.) Repeat with the second wrapper.

5. Using a metal spatula, carefully lift one of the packets from the work surface and slide the packet into the hot oil. Allow the turnover to cook, ladling some of the hot oil over the top, until puffed, crisp, and golden on both sides, 60 to 80 seconds. Quickly lift the turnover out of the hot oil and transfer it to a paper-towel-lined baking sheet to drain. Cook the second turnover. Then assemble the 2 remaining turnovers and cook them as described. Serve the turnovers hot, with additional harissa if desired.

It takes a bit of practice to make these turnovers. If the raw egg tries to run out of one of the sides before the edges of the wrapper are sealed, simply lift that edge to reposition the egg until you have sealed all the edges. The turnovers are forgiving and it really doesn't matter where the egg is situated inside the turnover as long as it gets sealed properly. The turnovers are best if assembled just before frying; otherwise the fragile wrappers tend to tear or burst while cooking. If you happen to have a sous-chef to help you in the kitchen, it works well to have one person assemble the turnovers while another person fries them. They cook so quickly that it takes about the same amount of time to assemble one as it does to cook one, making a tag team the best bet for efficiently assembling and cooking these delicious treats.

Note: Preserved lemons are available at most Middle Eastern grocery stores and at some gourmet markets.

# ORANGE AND HERB–ROASTED LAMB PITA

10 to 12 servings

Roasting a boneless leg of lamb is much easier than you think, and of course it makes an impressive dinner. You'll even have leftovers. If you're expecting a big crowd for lunch, this is just the right amount of meat, and it makes for a beautiful sandwich platter!

### Lamb

2 cups olive oil

Zest of 1 orange removed in strips with a vegetable peeler

½ cup freshly squeezed orange juice

½ cup orange blossom or other honey

¼ cup fresh rosemary leaves

¼ cup fresh marjoram leaves

2 tablespoons fresh thyme leaves

1 tablespoon crushed red pepper

4 cloves garlic, sliced

One 4-pound boneless leg of lamb, butterflied

⅓ cup toasted unsalted hazelnuts

¼ cup coriander seeds

1 tablespoon cumin seeds

1½ teaspoons fennel seeds

1½ teaspoons black peppercorns

1 tablespoon plus 1 teaspoon salt

Pitas

10 to 12 pita breads (see page 290)

Spiced Yogurt (page 322), for serving

3 cups chopped romaine lettuce

2 cups chopped fresh tomatoes

Classic Red Harissa (page 322), for serving

1. To cook the lamb: In a large mixing bowl, combine the olive oil, orange zest, orange juice, honey, rosemary, marjoram, thyme, crushed red pepper, and garlic. Place the lamb in a large resealable plastic food storage bag, and pour the olive oil mixture over it. Seal the bag and refrigerate the lamb for at least 24 hours (turn it over midway) and up to 36 hours.

2. In a spice grinder or using a mortar and pestle, combine the hazelnuts, coriander seeds, cumin seeds, fennel seeds, and peppercorns, and crush to a coarse consistency. Add 1 teaspoon of the salt and mix well. Set aside.

3. Remove the lamb from the refrigerator and let it rest at room temperature for at least 30 minutes and up to 1 hour.

4. Preheat the oven to 450°F.

5. Remove the lamb from the marinade and discard the marinade. Cut 3 long lengths of kitchen twine and lay them across a large cutting board. Position the lamb, fat side down, on top of the strings. Spread the hazelnut spice mixture over the lamb, and then season it with 2 teaspoons salt. Roll the meat up as tightly as you can, forming a cylinder, and tie it in three places to secure. Sprinkle the remaining 1 teaspoon salt all over the lamb, and place the lamb, seam side down, in a roasting pan.

6. Place the pan in the oven and immediately reduce the temperature to 350°F. Roast the lamb for 1 hour and 20 minutes, or until it registers 125° to 130°F on an instant-read thermometer. Begin checking the temperature after it has cooked for 1 hour, and continue to monitor the lamb to be sure it does not overcook. Once the lamb has come

to temperature, remove it from the oven and allow it to rest for at least 20 minutes before slicing. Then thinly slice the lamb across the grain.

7. To assemble: Cut the pitas in half and open them to form pockets. Stuff each pita pocket with several slices of lamb. Spoon some of the Spiced Yogurt over the meat, and then add lettuce, tomato, and harissa to taste.

# CURRIED POTATO AND DAL–FILLED SAMOSAS

18 samosas, 6 servings

Samosas make a great lunch, appetizer, or even just a snack. They reheat well in the oven, too. The potatoes and lentils themselves can be a dish all their own, as you will see, and the amounts are easily doubled. But go ahead, fill the dough and fry them first—these babies are delicious.

Pastry Dough (recipe follows)

All-purpose flour for dusting

Dal (recipe follows)

Curried Potatoes (recipe follows)

Vegetable oil, for frying

Tamarind Chutney (page 344), for serving

1. Cut the pastry dough into 9 equal pieces. Set 3 pieces on a lightly floured work surface and refrigerate the remaining dough, covered, until ready to use. (The dough is most easily handled when cold.)

2. Roll each piece of dough into a 6-inch round and then cut it in half. Spoon a generous teaspoon of dal on one end of each half-round. Top with a generous tablespoon of curried potato. Close the samosas by folding the opposite end of the half-round over and around the filling. Pinch the edges to seal. The samosas will roughly resemble a triangle. Set the samosas aside on a plate in the refrigerator, and repeat with the remaining dough and filling.

3. Set a cast-iron skillet or other heavy-bottomed pan over medium-high heat. Add oil to a depth of ½ inch, and heat it to 350°F. Add the samosas to the oil, a few at a time, and fry for 1 to 1½ minutes per side, or until golden. Remove them from the oil with a slotted spoon and transfer them to paper towels to drain. Serve immediately, with the Tamarind Chutney alongside.

# Pastry Dough

Enough for 18 samosas

1½ cups all-purpose flour

½ teaspoon salt

8 tablespoons (1 stick) cold unsalted butter, cut into cubes

⅓ cup ice water

1. Combine the flour, salt, and butter in the bowl of a food processor. Process for about 30 seconds, until the mixture resembles coarse crumbs. With the processor running, slowly drizzle in the ice water and continue to process until the dough gathers into a rough ball.

2. Transfer the dough to a lightly floured surface and form it into a disk. Wrap it in plastic wrap and let it rest in the refrigerator for at least 30 minutes and up to 2 days, or freeze it for up to 6 months.

# Dal

About 1½ cups

½ cup yellow split peas, rinsed and drained

2 cups water

½ teaspoon salt

¼ teaspoon ground turmeric

3 whole cloves

3 cardamom pods, cracked with your fingers

One 3-inch cinnamon stick

3 tablespoons butter

½ teaspoon cumin seeds

½ teaspoon fennel seeds

Pinch of crushed red pepper

¼ cup minced onion

1 teaspoon freshly squeezed lemon juice

1. In a small saucepan, combine the split peas, water, ¼ teaspoon of the salt, the turmeric, cloves, cardamom pods, and cinnamon stick. Bring to a simmer over medium heat. Then partially cover and cook for 45 minutes, or until the split peas are tender and the liquid has been absorbed. Remove from the heat. Remove and discard the cloves, cardamom pods, and cinnamon stick.

2. Melt the butter in a small saucepan. Add the cumin seeds, fennel seeds, crushed red pepper, onion, and the remaining ¼ teaspoon salt. Cook until the onion is soft, about 5 minutes.

3. Stir in the lemon juice. Pour this butter-onion mixture over the split peas, and stir to combine. Set aside until ready to use, or cover and refrigerate for up to 1 week.

# Curried Potatoes

2 pounds Idaho potatoes, peeled and cut into ½-inch dice

4 cups water

2½ teaspoons salt

4 tablespoons (½ stick) butter

½ cup chopped onion

½ teaspoon curry powder

¼ teaspoon crushed red pepper

½ cup frozen green peas

¼ cup chopped fresh cilantro leaves

1. Combine the potatoes, water, and 2 teaspoons of the salt in a medium saucepan, and bring to a boil over medium-high heat. Reduce the heat to a simmer and cook for 3 to 4 minutes, or until tender. Drain the potatoes.

2. Melt the butter in a 10-inch or larger sauté pan over medium heat. Add the onion, the remaining ½ teaspoon salt, the curry powder, and the crushed red pepper. Cook until the onion is soft and translucent, about 5 minutes. Add the drained potatoes, raise the heat to high, and cook, stirring as needed, until the potatoes are lightly browned, about 7 minutes. Add the peas and cilantro, toss to combine, and remove from the heat.

Croque Madame on a Croissant,
see pages 237–239

# BREAKFAST AND BRUNCH

# CHICKEN AND BISCUITS WITH REDEYE GRAVY

6 servings

This gravy is made with coffee—hence its name. Traditionally it's made with ham drippings too, served over ham, and sopped up with a biscuit. For a twist, I put it together with fried chicken. A breakfast sandwich never tasted so good.

1½ pounds boneless, skinless chicken thighs (trimmed of excess fat, if necessary)

1 cup evaporated milk

2 tablespoons freshly ground black pepper

2 teaspoons minced garlic

2 cups plus 2 tablespoons all-purpose flour

2½ teaspoons salt

Vegetable oil, for frying

1 small onion, finely chopped

¾ cup brewed coffee

¾ cup chicken stock or packaged low-sodium chicken broth, plus more if needed

¼ cup heavy cream

¼ cup chopped green onion

Cheddar and Green Onion Biscuits (recipe follows)

1. Place the chicken between two pieces of plastic wrap and use a mallet or the bottom of a heavy skillet to pound each piece to a thickness of about ¼ inch.

2. In a medium bowl, mix the evaporated milk, 1 tablespoon of the pepper, and the garlic. Add the chicken pieces, cover, and refrigerate for 4 hours or up to overnight.

3. In another medium bowl, combine the 2 cups flour with 2 teaspoons of the salt and 2 teaspoons of the black pepper. Remove the chicken from the marinade

(reserve the marinade). Lightly dredge the chicken pieces in the flour, shaking to remove the excess, dip them in the marinade, and then dredge them in the flour again. Set the chicken aside on a cooling rack or plate.

4. Fill a cast-iron skillet or other heavy-bottomed pot with vegetable oil to a depth of 1 inch, and heat it over medium-high heat to 350°F. Add a few pieces of the chicken to the pan and cook until browned on one side, about 3 minutes. While the chicken is cooking, continue to monitor the heat of the oil with a deep-frying thermometer, making sure the temperature stays between 330° and 350°F. Turn the chicken and cook on the other side for 3 to 4 minutes, until golden and cooked through. Remove the chicken from the pan and set it aside on a paper-towel-lined plate to drain. Repeat with the remaining chicken pieces.

5. Remove all but 2 tablespoons oil from the skillet, and add the onion. Cook over medium heat, stirring as needed and scraping up any browned bits in the pan, until the onion is soft and translucent, about 5 minutes. Add the remaining 2 tablespoons flour, stir well to combine, and cook for 2 minutes longer to make a roux. Whisk in the coffee and chicken stock, and cook until the sauce has thickened, about 6 minutes. Add the heavy cream, green onion, remaining 1 teaspoon pepper, and remaining ½ teaspoon salt, and cook for 2 to 3 minutes more, until the gravy reaches the desired consistency. If the sauce thickens too much, thin it with additional chicken stock.

6. To assemble: Slice a biscuit in half. Set a piece of fried chicken on the bottom half, spoon some of the gravy over the chicken, and top with the other half of the biscuit. Repeat with the remaining chicken, biscuits, and gravy. Serve immediately.

## Cheddar and Green Onion Biscuits

6 biscuits

1¼ cups self-rising flour
¾ cup cake flour

¾ teaspoon baking powder

⅛ teaspoon baking soda

1 tablespoon sugar

½ teaspoon salt

4 tablespoons (½ stick) cold unsalted butter,
    cut into pieces, plus 3 tablespoons melted

⅓ cup grated cheddar cheese

2 tablespoons chopped green onion tops

1½ cups heavy cream

¼ cup all-purpose flour, for dusting

1. Preheat the oven to 475°F.

2. Sift the self-rising flour, cake flour, baking powder, baking soda, sugar, and salt together into a large bowl. Using your fingers or a pastry cutter, work the cold butter into the flour until the pieces are pea size. Add the cheddar and green onions. Pour the heavy cream into the mixture, and with your hands or a rubber spatula, stir just until the cream and flour come together to form a dough.

3. Sprinkle some of the all-purpose flour on a work surface and place the dough on top of the flour. Using a lightly floured rolling pin or your hands, shape the dough into a ½-inch-thick disk about 8 inches in diameter. Using a sharp 3-inch round cutter dusted with flour, cut out 6 dough rounds. Be sure to press straight down when cutting the dough—a twisting motion will prevent the dough from rising.

4. Place the biscuits on an ungreased baking sheet and brush the tops with the melted butter. Bake until golden brown, 10 to 12 minutes.

# LYONNAISE SANDWICH

4 to 8 servings

The Lyonnaise salad is classic French bistro fare. Here I've deconstructed the salad and turned it into an open-face sandwich with bacon, eggs, and frisée lettuce. This sandwich is great any time of the day—perfect for breakfast or lunch and yet sophisticated enough to have for dinner.

1 bunch frisée lettuce, rinsed, spun dry, and roughly chopped

1 pound applewood-smoked bacon, cooked and crumbled into bite-size pieces

1 cup Dijon Vinaigrette (page 329)

¼ teaspoon sea salt or kosher salt, plus more for seasoning

Freshly ground black pepper, for seasoning

2 tablespoons butter

8 large eggs

8 slices crusty rustic bread, such as peasant bread or artisanal wheat bread, toasted

1 cup Herbed Aïoli (page 315)

1. In a large mixing bowl, toss the frisée and the bacon with some of the Dijon Vinaigrette, and season with the ¼ teaspoon salt and black pepper to taste.

2. In a large nonstick sauté pan, melt the butter over medium heat. Raise the heat to high, crack 2 of the eggs into the hot sauté pan, and season them lightly with salt and pepper. Fry the eggs for 2 to 3 minutes, until the yolk has almost set. (Cook the egg for less time for a runnier yolk.) Set aside on a plate. Repeat with the remaining eggs.

3. Spread 1 tablespoon of the Herbed Aïoli over each slice of toast. Divide the frisée salad among the 8 slices, and top each with a fried egg. Drizzle each sandwich with some of the remaining vinaigrette, and serve immediately.

# HERBED GOAT CHEESE AND EGG ON AN ENGLISH MUFFIN

4 to 6 servings

Making breakfast sandwiches at home is quick, easy, and inexpensive. The addition of herbed goat cheese (which can be prepared in advance) makes this simple sandwich seem extravagant and definitely puts other ones to shame.

4 ounces soft mild goat cheese, at room temperature

1½ tablespoons chopped fresh chives

1 teaspoon chopped fresh tarragon leaves

2 tablespoons unsalted butter

2 ounces finely chopped sliced Black Forest ham (or other quality smoked ham, such as Smithfield, Westphalian, or Virginia)

6 eggs

3 tablespoons milk

½ teaspoon salt

¼ teaspoon freshly ground black pepper

4 to 6 English Muffins (page 277) or crumpets, split and lightly toasted

Grated Parmigiano-Reggiano cheese, for garnish

1. In a small bowl, combine the goat cheese with 1 tablespoon of the chives and the tarragon. Set aside, or cover and refrigerate for up to 1 week.

2. Heat a large nonstick sauté pan over medium-high heat. When it is hot, add 1 tablespoon of the butter, and when it begins to bubble, add the ham. Cook the ham for 1 to 2 minutes, until it is just golden brown. Using a slotted spoon, transfer the

ham to a paper-towel-lined plate and set it aside. Wipe the pan clean and return it to the stove.

3. Combine the eggs, milk, salt, and pepper in a medium mixing bowl and whisk well to combine.

4. Heat the sauté pan over medium heat, and add the remaining 1 tablespoon butter. Once the butter has melted, add the eggs to the pan. Allow the eggs to set for 30 seconds; then begin stirring slowly with a heat-resistant rubber spatula. As soon as curds begin to form, raise the heat to high and instead of stirring, use the spatula to fold the eggs over themselves. Fold in the goat cheese and the ham, and cook for another 45 seconds, or until warmed through.

5. Divide the eggs evenly among the English muffins, and garnish with the remaining ½ tablespoon chopped chives and grated Parmesan to taste. Serve immediately.

# MASCARPONE AND MARMALADE–STUFFED FRENCH TOAST

4 sandwiches

Whoa, Nelly. This could be the mother of all French toast, and it is to die for. Did you ever imagine it stuffed? Well, just think of it as a yummy grilled cheese dessert sandwich for breakfast. Move over, doughnuts.

6 large eggs

½ cup heavy cream

Juice of ½ orange

1½ teaspoons grated orange zest

½ teaspoon ground cinnamon

¼ teaspoon freshly grated nutmeg

½ teaspoon vanilla extract

3 tablespoons sugar

¼ teaspoon salt

¼ cup plus 2 tablespoons mascarpone cheese

3 tablespoons orange marmalade

Eight ¾-inch-thick slices day-old brioche, homemade (see page 272), or store-bought

2 tablespoons butter

Confectioners' sugar, for dusting

Maple syrup, for serving

1. In a mixing bowl, whisk together the eggs, cream, orange juice, orange zest, cinnamon, nutmeg, vanilla, sugar, and salt.

2. Place the mascarpone in a small bowl. Place the marmalade in another small bowl.

3. Lay the brioche slices on a clean work surface. Spread the mascarpone evenly over the slices. Spread the marmalade evenly over half of the slices. (You will have mascarpone on both sides of the sandwich and marmalade on one side.) Place the slices together to form 4 sandwiches.

4. Dip each sandwich in the egg mixture, letting it sit for about 1½ minutes per side. Transfer it to a plate and repeat with the remaining sandwiches.

5. Heat a large nonstick skillet over low heat. Add 1 tablespoon of the butter. When the butter has melted, add 2 of the sandwiches and cook until golden brown on both sides, about 5 minutes per side. Repeat with the remaining 1 tablespoon butter and remaining 2 sandwiches.

6. Cut the French toast sandwiches in half and serve hot, dusted with confectioners' sugar and drizzled with maple syrup, as desired.

# BREAKFAST BURRITO WITH CHORIZO, BLACK BEANS, AND AVOCADO CREMA

4 burritos

Everyone should be so lucky as to have breakfast like this every day! Spicy, savory sausage and black beans come together with scrambled eggs and creamy Avocado Crema—*mmmmm,* so satisfying.

4 large flour tortillas

2 cups drained cooked black beans
(about two 14-ounce cans)

½ cup chicken stock or
packaged low-sodium chicken broth

1 pound fresh chorizo sausage (or other spicy sausage),
removed from the casings

1 cup small-diced onion

¼ cup small-diced red bell pepper

¼ cup small-diced green bell pepper

1 teaspoon minced garlic

2 teaspoons salt, plus more for seasoning

½ teaspoon freshly ground black pepper

8 large eggs

3 tablespoons heavy cream

1 tablespoon olive oil

1 cup shredded Monterey Jack cheese (about 4 ounces)

1 cup Avocado Crema (page 332), for serving

Red Onion and Tomato Salsa Fresca (page 328)
or your favorite salsa, for serving

1. Position an oven rack in the center and preheat the oven to 200°F.

2. Stack the tortillas and wrap them in foil. Place them in the oven to warm until ready to use.

3. In a small mixing bowl, thoroughly mash ¼ cup of the black beans with the back of a fork. Stir in the chicken stock and mix well. Set aside.

4. Heat a 12-inch sauté pan over medium-high heat. Add the chorizo and cook until browned, about 5 minutes, stirring occasionally and breaking it into small pieces. Add the onion, bell peppers, garlic, and a pinch of salt, and cook until the vegetables soften, 3 to 4 minutes. Add the remaining whole black beans, the mashed bean mixture, 1 teaspoon of the salt, and ¼ teaspoon of the black pepper. Stir to mix well. Cook until most of the liquid has evaporated, about 1 minute. Remove from the heat and cover to keep warm.

5. In a medium bowl, whisk together the eggs, cream, remaining 1 teaspoon salt, and remaining ¼ teaspoon black pepper. In a small nonstick sauté pan, heat the olive oil over medium heat. Add the eggs, and using a heat-resistant rubber spatula, immediately begin stirring and shaking the pan simultaneously (remove the pan from the heat as necessary so that the eggs don't brown), cooking until the eggs are curdled but still wet, about 1½ minutes. Remove from the heat and set aside.

6. Remove the tortillas from the oven. Place a tortilla on a work surface and sprinkle ¼ cup of the cheese down the center of the tortilla. Spoon ½ cup of the sausage and black beans over the cheese. Add one-quarter of the scrambled eggs. Spread ¼ cup of the Avocado Crema on top of the eggs. Fold one or both ends of the burrito in, and then roll the burrito as snugly as you can to form a cylinder. Repeat with the remaining tortillas. Serve immediately, with Red Onion and Tomato Salsa Fresca alongside.

# EMERIL'S SMOKED SALMON BAGEL WITH MASCARPONE SPREAD

4 sandwiches

This is on the menu at my flagship restaurant, Emeril's, in New Orleans. Simple, yet *sooo* delicious. The mascarpone makes a great alternative to cream cheese, and the capers are a classic complement to the smoked salmon. *Tip:* Let the bagels cool off a bit after you toast 'em before adding the mascarpone, so it doesn't melt too much.

1 pound mascarpone cheese, at room temperature

¼ cup plus 2 tablespoons nonpareil capers, drained and roughly chopped

Finely grated zest of 2 lemons

½ teaspoon salt

¼ teaspoon freshly ground white pepper

4 sesame bagels, halved and lightly toasted

8 ounces sliced smoked salmon

½ cup thinly sliced red onion (⅛-inch-thick) rounds

Eight ¼-inch-thick tomato slices

1. Place the mascarpone, capers, lemon zest, salt, and white pepper in a mixing bowl and stir to combine. Spread about 3 tablespoons of the mixture onto each bagel half.

2. Divide the salmon slices among the bottom halves of the bagels; follow with the sliced onion and the tomato slices. Place the top half of the bagels over the tomatoes. Serve immediately.

# POACHED EGGS WITH PROSCIUTTO-WRAPPED ASPARAGUS AND BÉARNAISE SAUCE

8 open-face sandwiches, 4 to 8 servings

This is my kicked-up version of Eggs Benedict—serve this at your next brunch to really wow your guests. You can simplify things by wrapping the asparagus up to one day ahead. The béarnaise sauce is made in the blender and can be prepared up to an hour in advance.

3 quarts water

1 cup white wine vinegar

8 large eggs

1 bunch large asparagus, woody portion of the stems removed

¼ teaspoon salt, plus more for seasoning

⅛ teaspoon freshly ground black pepper, plus more for seasoning

2 ounces very thinly sliced prosciutto

1 tablespoon olive oil

4 English Muffins (page 277), split and toasted

Béarnaise Sauce (page 346), for serving

1. Preheat the oven to 350°F.

2. In a large saucepan, bring the water to a boil over high heat. Add the vinegar, immediately reduce the heat, and keep the water at a simmer.

3. Meanwhile, crack the eggs into small individual bowls and set them aside.

4. Season the asparagus with the ¼ teaspoon salt and the ⅛ teaspoon pepper. Wrap each spear of asparagus with a slice of prosciutto, starting just below the tip of the asparagus and ending about ½ inch from the bottom.

5. Heat a 14-inch ovenproof sauté pan over medium-high heat. When it is hot, add the olive oil and the asparagus and cook, shaking the pan, until the prosciutto is golden brown, about 6 minutes. Place the pan in the oven and bake for 5 minutes, or until the asparagus is fork-tender. Remove the asparagus from the oven, cover it loosely with aluminum foil to keep warm, and set aside.

6. Working in batches of 2 or 3, slip the eggs, one at time, into the simmering water and cook them for about 3 minutes, or until they have become opaque and the whites are coagulated. Carefully remove the eggs with a slotted spoon and set them aside on a paper-towel-lined plate. Season them with salt and pepper.

7. To assemble: Place 3 prosciutto-wrapped asparagus spears on each half of a toasted English muffin. Top the asparagus with a poached egg, and then ladle 2 tablespoons béarnaise sauce over the top. Serve immediately.

# BREAKFAST BURGER

4 sandwiches

Don't you sometimes want a good burger to wake you up and get you going? Here's the solution: killer hash brown potatoes, a big breakfast sausage patty, and cheese, sandwiched between pieces of French toast. If you want, use biscuits instead and add eggs as you please.

### Hash browns

2 pounds Idaho potatoes

1 onion, chopped

1 teaspoon salt

½ teaspoon freshly ground black pepper

1½ tablespoons chopped fresh thyme leaves

2 tablespoons vegetable oil

2 tablespoons butter

¼ cup heavy cream

### Sausage patties

1 pound bulk breakfast sausage

### French toast

¾ cup whole milk

3 large eggs

¼ teaspoon salt

Eight ¼-inch-thick slices day-old brioche rolls (see page 272), or
    other soft rolls about 4 inches in diameter

4 tablespoons (½ stick) butter

4 ounces sliced cheddar, Jack and Colby mix, or American cheese

1. To make the hash browns: Peel the potatoes and grate them on the large holes of a box grater or using the large grating disk on a food processor. In two batches, rinse the potatoes and wring them dry in a kitchen towel. Combine the potatoes, onion, salt, black pepper, and thyme in a mixing bowl, and mix well.

2. Heat the oil in a well-seasoned 10-inch cast-iron skillet over medium heat. Add the butter, and when it has melted, add the potato mixture. Spread the potato mixture out, press it evenly in the skillet with a metal spatula, and cook for 5 minutes. Then shake the skillet to loosen the potatoes from the bottom, press the potatoes again, and continue to cook until they are nicely browned on the bottom, about 10 minutes longer. Using the metal spatula, cut the potatoes into 4 parts, and flip them over. Press the potatoes in the skillet and cook for 5 minutes. Then add the cream and continue to cook until the liquid has been absorbed and the potatoes have developed a nice crust on the bottom, about 10 minutes. At this point most of the bottom surface of the potatoes should be crusted; if not, continue to cook a bit longer, pressing with your spatula to encourage crusting. Remove the potatoes from the skillet and set them aside until cool enough to handle. Once they have cooled, cut them into 4 rounds with a 4-inch-diameter biscuit cutter (eat the leftover edges, of course). (Alternatively, form the hash browns into 4-inch patties with your hands once they are cool enough to handle.)

3. To make the sausage patties: While the potatoes are cooking, divide the sausage into 4 patties and press them into the size and shape of the bread slices, about 4 inches in diameter. Cook the sausage according to package directions, and set aside.

4. Preheat the oven to 400°F.

5. To make the French toast: In a shallow pan, whisk together the milk, eggs, and salt. Add several slices of the brioche and allow them to soak on both sides for about 3 minutes total. Heat a medium skillet over medium heat, and melt 2 tablespoons of the

butter in it. Add the soaked bread and cook until golden brown on each side, about 3 minutes total. Remove from the pan and set aside. Repeat with the remaining bread and remaining 2 tablespoons butter.

6. To assemble: Set a hash brown round on one of the French toast slices, top with a slice of cheese, add a sausage patty, and top with another slice of French toast. Repeat with the remaining ingredients. Place the sandwiches on a baking sheet and bake in the oven until the cheese is melted and the burger is warmed through, 4 to 6 minutes. Serve immediately.

# CROQUE MADAME ON A CROISSANT

4 sandwiches

This sandwich is the perfect candidate for breakfast champion: a buttery crisp croissant loaded with Black Forest ham and cheese, topped with a Parmesan béchamel and a fried egg. Whoa! This will get your day started right.

4 tablespoons unsalted butter

2 tablespoons all-purpose flour

1 cup whole milk

½ teaspoon salt, plus more for seasoning

⅛ teaspoon freshly grated nutmeg

⅛ teaspoon cayenne pepper

3 tablespoons finely grated Parmigiano-Reggiano cheese

4 large eggs

Freshly ground black pepper

4 croissants

8 ounces thinly sliced Black Forest ham
    (or another quality smoked ham, such as
    Smithfield, Westphalian, or Virginia)

1 cup grated Gruyère cheese

1 teaspoon chopped fresh thyme leaves

1 teaspoon chopped fresh chives

1. Melt 2 tablespoons of the butter in a small saucepan over medium heat. When it has melted, add the flour and stir for 1½ to 2 minutes. Gradually whisk in the milk. Raise the heat to medium-high and bring to a simmer. Add the salt, nutmeg,

cayenne, and Parmesan, and whisk to combine. Cook for 3 minutes, whisking constantly until the sauce thickens. Remove the béchamel sauce from the heat and set it aside.

2. Position an oven rack in the upper third of the oven and preheat the broiler.

3. In a large nonstick sauté pan, melt the remaining 2 tablespoons butter over medium heat. Once the butter has melted, raise the heat to high, crack 2 of the eggs into the hot sauté pan, and season them lightly with salt and pepper. Fry the eggs for 2 to 3 minutes, or until the yolk has almost set. (Cook the egg for less time for a runnier yolk.) Set the fried eggs aside on a plate. Repeat with the remaining eggs.

4. Slice the croissants in half and place the bottom halves on a baking sheet. Place 2 slices of ham on each bottom half, and place ¼ cup of the Gruyère on top of each portion of ham. Broil for 1 to 2 minutes, just until the cheese has melted.

5. Top with the remaining halves of the croissants. Ladle 2 tablespoons of the béchamel on top of each sandwich, sprinkle each sandwich with ¼ teaspoon thyme and ¼ teaspoon chives, and place a fried egg on top of the béchamel. Serve immediately.

Chocolate Wafers
with Peanut Butter
Fudge, see pages
264–266

# Sweet

## SANDWICHES

# ANGEL CAKE SANDWICHES WITH FRESH BERRIES AND CRÈME CHANTILLY

*12 sandwiches*

This recipe is a riff on old-fashioned strawberry shortcake, made a little lighter with angel food cake in place of the more traditional biscuits. These little babies are super easy to make but so impressive that you'll have folks thinking you worked all day.

12 egg whites

1 teaspoon cream of tartar

1½ cups plus 2 tablespoons superfine sugar

3 teaspoons vanilla extract

¼ teaspoon almond extract

1 cup cake flour

1 cup heavy cream

¼ cup confectioners' sugar

2 cups fresh berries, such as raspberries, blueberries, or blackberries

1. Preheat the oven to 375°F. Line the bottom of an 11¾ x 7½-inch jelly roll pan with parchment paper.

2. Place the egg whites and the cream of tartar in the bowl of a standing mixer fitted with the whisk attachment, and beat until the whites form soft peaks. Add ¾ cup of the superfine sugar in a slow, steady stream while beating at medium speed. Add 2 teaspoons of the vanilla extract and the almond extract. Continue to beat the whites until they become glossy and maintain a stiff peak.

3. Combine ¾ cup of the superfine sugar and the flour in a bowl, and sift twice. Sift a third time over the egg whites. Using a spatula, gently fold the flour mixture into the egg whites, taking care that the flour is fully incorporated.

4. Pour the batter onto the prepared jelly roll pan and bake for 20 minutes, or until the top is lightly golden and the cake springs back when touched lightly with your finger. Remove the pan from the oven and place it on a wire rack to cool. Once the cake has cooled completely, invert the pan onto a large cutting board or other work surface. Remove the pan, leaving the parchment paper attached to the cake.

5. In the bowl of the electric mixer, combine the heavy cream, confectioners' sugar, and remaining 1 teaspoon vanilla extract. Beat for 2 to 3 minutes, until soft peaks form. Set aside.

6. In a small mixing bowl, combine the berries with the remaining 2 tablespoons superfine sugar, and stir gently until the sugar has dissolved.

7. Remove the parchment from the angel food cake, and using a 2-inch round cookie cutter, cut the cake into 24 rounds.

8. Turn all the cake rounds so that the golden side is on the bottom and the bright white side faces up. Spoon 3 or 4 berries on top of 12 cakes, and then spoon 1 tablespoon of the whipped cream on top of the berries. Place the remaining cake rounds on top, white side up, and dollop with another spoonful of the whipped cream. Garnish the top of each sandwich with a berry, and serve immediately.

# SWEETENED CREAM CHEESE AND CHERRY JAM TURNOVERS

8 turnovers

One secret to a delicious turnover is the quality of jam you use; make sure you buy a good one—it makes all the difference. Also, if you don't like cherry, the good news is that you can use any jam you like!

¾ cup (6 ounces) cream cheese, at room temperature

3 tablespoons sugar

¼ cup ricotta cheese

1 large egg yolk

1 teaspoon vanilla extract

⅛ teaspoon salt

2 sheets frozen puff pastry, thawed according to package instructions

All-purpose flour, for dusting

2 tablespoons plus 2 teaspoons cherry jam

1 large egg

1 tablespoon water

1. Place the cream cheese and sugar in the bowl of a standing mixer fitted with the paddle attachment, and cream on low speed until smooth. Add the ricotta, egg yolk, vanilla, and salt, and continue to mix until well combined. Using a rubber spatula, transfer the mixture to a small bowl. Cover it with plastic wrap and refrigerate.

2. Unfold one of the pastry sheets on a floured work surface. Roll out the pastry to form a 12-inch square that is ⅛ inch thick; trim it with a knife to make clean, even

edges. Divide the square into four 6-inch squares and set them aside. Repeat with the remaining pastry sheet.

3. Arrange the squares so that they look like diamonds, with a corner toward you. On each square, place 2 tablespoons of the cream cheese mixture near the center, and then spread it along the bottom of the diamond, leaving about ½ inch of space along the edges. Add 1 teaspoon of cherry jam on top of the cream cheese.

4. In a small bowl, whisk the egg and water together to create an egg wash. Lightly brush the edges of each pastry diamond with the egg wash.

5. To form the turnovers, fold the top corner over the bottom to create a triangle. Make sure the corners and edges meet evenly, and then lightly press them together. To seal, use the tines of a fork to press about ¼ inch in along the edges. When you have formed all the turnovers, lightly brush the tops and edges with the egg wash. Cut two small diagonal slits in the top of each turnover to allow steam to escape during cooking.

6. Line two baking sheets with parchment paper and place 4 turnovers on each sheet, leaving about an inch of space between them. Refrigerate until chilled, about 1 hour.

7. Position an oven rack in the center and preheat the oven to 425°F.

8. One baking sheet at a time, bake the turnovers until they are golden brown and puffy, rotating the sheet midway through cooking, about 16 minutes total. Remove the baking sheets from the oven and set the sheets aside on a wire rack to cool briefly before serving, about 10 minutes. Serve warm or at room temperature.

# GINGER ICE CREAM SANDWICHES WITH GINGER MOLASSES COOKIES

6 to 8 sandwiches

Ice cream sandwiches are the quintessential dessert sandwich and are loved by children and adults alike. Make a batch of these and store them, individually wrapped, in the freezer; they're perfect for an anytime treat.

### Ginger ice cream

1 cup whole milk

1 cup granulated sugar

¼ cup chopped fresh ginger

1½ teaspoons vanilla extract

2 cups heavy cream

Pinch of salt

### Cookies

2 cups all-purpose flour

1 teaspoon baking soda

1½ teaspoons ground ginger

¼ teaspoon ground cinnamon

¼ teaspoon ground cardamom

⅛ teaspoon sea salt

12 tablespoons (1½ sticks) unsalted butter,
    at room temperature

½ cup packed dark brown sugar

½ cup granulated sugar

¼ cup unsulphured molasses

1 large egg

2 teaspoons vanilla extract

3 tablespoons candied ginger

1. To make the ice cream: Combine the milk, granulated sugar, and ginger in a medium saucepan and bring to a boil. Immediately reduce the heat and simmer until the sugar has fully dissolved, about 5 minutes. Remove from the heat and add the vanilla, heavy cream, and salt. Let cool, and then transfer the mixture to a container, cover, and refrigerate until thoroughly chilled, at least 4 hours and up to 24 hours.

2. Churn the mixture in an ice cream maker according to the manufacturer's directions. Allow the ice cream to further harden, at least 2 hours, in the freezer before assembling the ice cream sandwiches.

3. To make the cookies: In a medium bowl, sift together the flour, baking soda, ginger, cinnamon, cardamom, and sea salt. Set aside.

4. In the bowl of a standing mixer fitted with the paddle attachment, combine the butter with the dark and granulated sugars on medium speed until light and fluffy. Turn the machine off, add the molasses, and then beat until fully incorporated. Add the egg and vanilla, scraping down the sides of the bowl as necessary, and continue to beat until blended. Reduce the mixer speed to low and add the flour mixture, one-third at a time, beating until blended. Transfer the dough to a piece of parchment paper, and roll it to form a 2-inch-wide cylinder. Refrigerate, covered with parchment, for at least 30 minutes and up to overnight.

5. Position a rack in the center of the oven, and preheat the oven to 350°F. Line two baking sheets with parchment paper.

6. Using a spice grinder, process the candied ginger until it is granulated (or finely mince it using your knife). Set aside.

7. Slice the dough into ¼-inch-thick rounds, and place them on the prepared baking sheets. Sprinkle the cookies with the candied ginger. Bake, one sheet at a time, for 10 to 12 minutes. Remove the cookies from the oven, transfer them to a wire rack, and cool completely.

8. Sandwich ½ cup of the ice cream between 2 cookies. Repeat with the remaining ice cream and cookies.

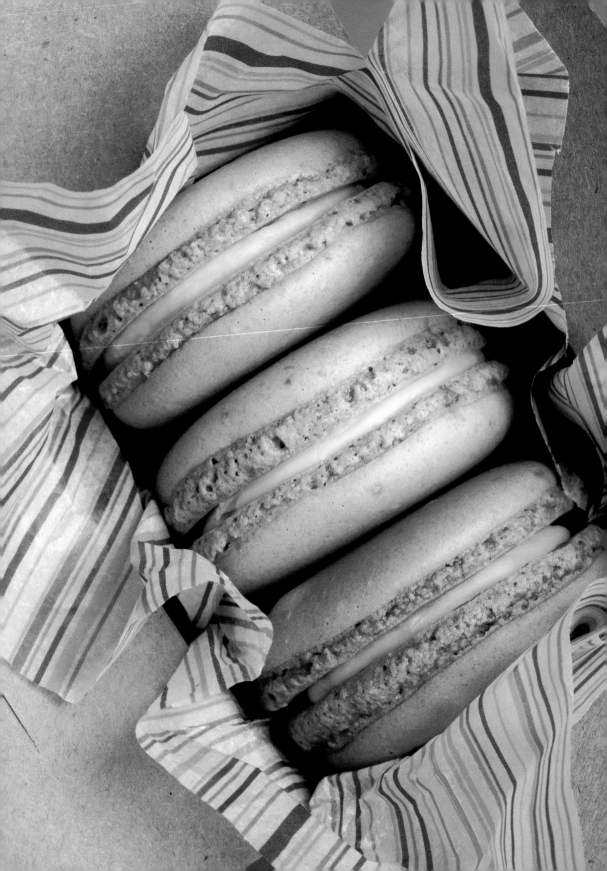

# CAFÉ AU LAIT MACARONS WITH WHITE CHOCOLATE GANACHE

About 30 macarons

These lovely cookies are as delicious as they look. With a crispy eggshell-like exterior and a chewy center with a creamy filling, it all comes together in one bite. The crinkled bottom edge on these Parisian treats is called the "foot," or in French, *le pied*. Perfectionists will obsess over obtaining this physical attribute, but I say, hey, if you don't get it the first time and they taste great, don't worry about it. The key to Parisian macarons is patience and practice, because truth be told, they can be temperamental. But they are completely worth it.

1 cup almond flour

1½ cups confectioners' sugar

1 tablespoon plus 1 teaspoon instant espresso powder
    (preferably Medaglia D'Oro)

3 large egg whites, at room temperature

Pinch of salt

2½ tablespoons granulated sugar

White Chocolate Ganache (recipe follows)

1. Position an oven rack in the center of the oven, and preheat the oven to 350°F.

2. Trim parchment paper to fit three large baking sheets. Create a stencil for piping the macarons by drawing 1-inch-diameter circles 1½ inches apart on the parchment (you should end up with about 24 circles per sheet). Place each piece of parchment

on a baking sheet, drawn side facing down. Place a second baking sheet under each parchment-covered sheet (you will need 6 sheets altogether).

3. Place the almond flour, confectioners' sugar, and espresso powder in a food processor and pulse until finely ground. Sift the mixture, and set it aside.

4. In the bowl of a standing mixer fitted with the whisk attachment, combine the egg whites and salt on low speed. Gradually increase to high speed, mixing until the egg whites become foamy, about 2 minutes. Then reduce the speed to low and add the granulated sugar, a tablespoon at a time. Return the speed to high and whisk until stiff, glossy peaks form, 1 to 2 minutes (if it looks clumpy or dry, you've gone too far). Remove the bowl from the mixer and place it on a work surface.

5. Add the almond flour mixture, in thirds, to the egg whites, gently folding it into the meringue (it will be streaky each time you add it). Once the flour mixture has been incorporated, spread the batter against the sides of the bowl; run the spatula under the batter and fold it over. Repeat this until the batter is shiny, feels slightly firm, and drips slowly from the spatula. When the batter drips back into the bowl and the peak disappears within 5 seconds, you have worked it to the right consistency. This is a crucial step and is referred to as *macaronage.*

6. Attach a ½-inch round tip to a pastry bag. Fill the pastry bag with the batter, and pipe the batter onto the stenciled circles, forming peaked mounds the size of a silver dollar. (The third baking sheet will not completely fill up—only about halfway.) Tap the baking sheets firmly against the counter to release any trapped air.

7. One baking sheet at a time, bake the macarons until the shells are slightly crisped on top, 18 minutes, rotating the sheet midway. Remove from the oven and set the baking sheets on a cooling rack.

8. When the macarons are completely cool, remove them from the baking sheets and pair each one with another of an equal size (you may need an offset spatula to help lift them off the paper). Squeeze a bit of the ganache onto one side of half the cookies, and top with the remaining cookies, pressing gently. Store in the refrigerator for a

couple of hours to set, or store them in an airtight container in the freezer for up to 2 weeks. Let thaw before serving.

## White Chocolate Ganache

Enough for 30 cookies

One 5.5-ounce premium-quality white chocolate bar, finely chopped

3 tablespoons heavy cream

1 tablespoon unsalted butter, cut into small dice, at room temperature

1 tablespoon nut-flavored liqueur, such as Nocello or Frangelico (optional)

Place the white chocolate in a small bowl. Heat the heavy cream in a very small saucepan over medium heat until it just comes to a boil (or microwave in a glass measuring cup). Remove from the heat and pour the hot cream over the chocolate. Let sit for 1 to 2 minutes. Then add the butter and liqueur (if using), and whisk until completely smooth. Transfer the ganache to a piping bag and let it set in the refrigerator for at least 4 hours or up to overnight.

# ALMOND–POPPY SEED POUND CAKE WITH LEMON NEUFCHÂTEL

8 servings

Tart and creamy Neufchâtel filling is sandwiched between lovely slices of cake. I warn you, it's very hard to eat only what you're served. So though this recipe is for eight, it can be devoured by four, especially if you have friends like mine who will slink into the kitchen when you're not looking.

12 tablespoons (1½ sticks) unsalted butter,
    at room temperature, plus more for greasing the pan
1½ cups granulated sugar
3 large eggs, at room temperature
1½ cups sifted cake flour
1 teaspoon almond extract
2 tablespoons plus 1 teaspoon poppy seeds
1 cup confectioners' sugar
3 tablespoons plus 1 teaspoon freshly squeezed lemon juice
Lemon Neufchâtel (recipe follows)

1. Preheat the oven to 350°F. Grease with butter and lightly flour an 8½ x 4½-inch loaf pan.

2. In the bowl of a standing mixer fitted with the paddle attachment, cream the butter on low speed for 1 minute. Slowly add the granulated sugar, and continue to mix until light and fluffy, about 5 minutes. Add 1 egg, and when it is completely incorporated, add one-third of the flour. Mix for 30 seconds. Repeat with the remaining eggs and flour. Add the almond extract and the poppy seeds, and mix for 30 seconds more, until evenly distributed. Scrape the bowl with a rubber spatula and transfer the batter to the prepared loaf pan.

3. Bake for 35 minutes. Then rotate the pan and continue to bake for another 35 to 40 minutes, until a toothpick inserted in one of the cracks has a trace of crumb. Remove the cake from the oven, set the pan on a wire rack, and let it cool for 10 minutes.

4. In a small bowl, whisk together the confectioners' sugar and lemon juice until smooth.

5. Run a thin metal spatula around the edges of the cake to loosen it from the pan, and place a wire rack or a plate on top. Carefully invert the cake onto the rack and lift off the loaf pan. Set another wire rack on the bottom of the cake, and turn it right side up. Set the rack over a parchment-lined baking sheet, and drizzle the lemon glaze over the top of the warm cake. Using a rubber spatula, smooth the glaze around the sides of the cake. You can scrape up any glaze that has dripped onto the parchment and drizzle back onto the cake. Allow the cake to cool completely before slicing, about 2 hours.

6. To assemble: Cut the cake into ½-inch-thick slices. Spread the Lemon Neufchâtel between 2 slices, forming a cake sandwich.

## Lemon Neufchâtel

1 cup

8 ounces Neufchâtel or cream cheese, at room temperature

2 tablespoons confectioners' sugar

1 teaspoon finely grated lemon zest

1½ teaspoons freshly squeezed lemon juice

Combine the Neufchâtel, confectioners' sugar, lemon zest, and lemon juice in a small bowl, and blend well with a rubber spatula or spoon. Use at room temperature. (Cover and refrigerate any unused portion for up to 1 week.)

# RED VELVET WHOOPIE PIES

18 whoopie pies

Whoopie pies have made a major comeback in the world of desserts. I can see why—they're reminiscent of some of my favorite childhood snack cakes. The tender cake sandwiches a sweet marshmallow creme filling that both children and adults will love. This recipe was tested and retested, mainly because everyone loved eating them so much and they're fun to make.

## Mini cakes

2 cups all-purpose flour

½ cup unsweetened cocoa powder

1 teaspoon baking soda

¼ teaspoon salt

8 tablespoons (1 stick) unsalted butter, at room temperature

1 cup granulated sugar

1 large egg

2 tablespoons red food coloring

1½ teaspoons vanilla extract

1 cup buttermilk (see Note, page 64)

## Filling

1½ cups confectioners' sugar

One 7-ounce container marshmallow creme

4 ounces cream cheese, at room temperature

2 tablespoons unsalted butter, at room temperature

1 teaspoon vanilla extract

1. To make the mini cakes: Preheat the oven to 400°F. Using cooking spray, grease two 11¾ x 17½-inch jelly roll pans. Set the pans aside.

2. In a medium mixing bowl, combine the flour, cocoa powder, baking soda, and salt. Set aside.

3. In the bowl of a standing mixer fitted with the paddle attachment, or in a medium mixing bowl, cream together the butter and granulated sugar. Add the egg and mix until it is fully incorporated. Add the red food coloring and the vanilla, and beat until well blended. Scrape the sides and bottom of the bowl and mix again. In thirds, alternately add the buttermilk and the flour mixture, beginning with the buttermilk and ending with the flour. Mix until the ingredients are just combined.

4. Place half of the batter in a piping bag fitted with a plain tip, and pipe twelve 2½-inch-diameter cookies onto the prepared jelly roll pans, spacing them 2 inches apart. Moisten your fingertip with water and smooth the top of each cookie. Bake the cookies, one pan at a time, for 6 minutes, or until they have puffed up. Allow the cookies to cool on the pan for 1 minute, and then transfer them to a wire rack to cool completely.

5. To make the filling: Combine the confectioners' sugar, marshmallow creme, cream cheese, butter, and vanilla in the bowl of a standing mixer fitted with the paddle attachment and mix until well blended. (You can make this filling up to 24 hours in advance.) Cover and refrigerate.

6. To assemble the cookies; Spread 1 tablespoon of the filling over half of the cookies, and top with the remaining cookies.

# PISTACHIO AND ALMOND GELATO ON BRIOCHE BUNS

About 1 quart ice cream, enough for 8 to 10 sandwiches

This is a typical treat in Sicily, where it gets really hot, and having gelato in brioche is the perfect remedy. They enjoy it any time of day there—even for breakfast! I make this pistachio-almond gelato for you—Sicilian style all the way, baby—by thickening it with cornstarch, resulting in a lighter gelato. I recommend making the brioche yourself and forming it into traditional rolls. However, if you don't feel like cranking up the oven, just purchase some quality brioche rolls (or any other soft, sweet roll), make the delicious gelato, and you're there.

1½ cups plus 2 tablespoons shelled unsalted pistachios

1½ cups plus 2 tablespoons slivered blanched almonds

4 cups whole milk

¾ cup superfine sugar

3 tablespoons cornstarch

2 pinches salt

½ teaspoon almond extract

8 to 10 Brioche Buns, homemade (page 272), or store-bought

1. Position an oven rack in the center of the oven, and preheat the oven to 350°F.

2. Spread the pistachios and almonds onto separate baking sheets lined with parchment paper. Toast the nuts in the oven until they are fragrant and golden, rotating the baking sheets midway, about 15 minutes total. Set aside to cool.

3. Roughly chop 2 tablespoons of the pistachios and 2 tablespoons of the almonds, and combine them in a small bowl. Set aside.

4. Process the remaining pistachios and almonds in a food processor until they're finely chopped (but not powdered).

5. Combine the finely chopped nuts and 3 cups of the milk in a saucepan, and bring just to a boil over medium heat; turn off the heat.

6. In a small bowl, combine the sugar and cornstarch, and whisk in the remaining 1 cup milk. Add the mixture to the saucepan and return it to medium heat. Bring to a boil and continue to cook until thickened, stirring as needed, about 8 minutes.

7. Meanwhile, fill a large bowl with ice and cold water.

8. Remove the saucepan from the stove and place it in the ice bath. Let the ice cream base cool, stirring it occasionally. When the ice cream base is just cooled, strain it through a chinois or other fine-mesh sieve into a bowl, using a ladle or wooden spoon to press on the nuts, extracting as much liquid as possible. Use a rubber spatula to scrape any excess ice cream base off the bottom of the chinois. Discard the nuts.

9. Whisk in the salt and almond extract, cover the bowl, and store in the refrigerator until thoroughly chilled, at least 4 hours and up to overnight.

10. Freeze in an ice cream maker according to the manufacturer's instructions. Fold in the reserved roughly chopped nuts, transfer to a freezer container, and freeze for 3 to 4 hours to set. (If you don't use the ice cream right away, you can store it in an airtight container in the freezer for up to 2 weeks.)

11. To assemble: Halve a brioche bun, and sandwich a scoop of the gelato between the halves. Repeat with the remaining ingredients. Serve immediately.

# DATE AND WALNUT POCKETS

About 24 cookies

These cookies are based on the Syrian and Lebanese cookie *mamoul* or *ma'amoul*. They are often stuffed with either a walnut or date puree, scented with either orange-flower water or rose water. The filling is sandwiched between a shortbread of sorts, often made with semolina flour. I've changed things up a bit here, using both dates and walnuts. I opted for a shortbread made with flour, cream cheese, and confectioners' sugar to make the cookie a little lighter and somewhat flaky. And hey, feel free to experiment with a variety of nuts or none at all.

8 ounces pitted Medjool or Noor dates, chopped

½ to ¾ cup water

½ cup finely chopped walnuts

2 tablespoons honey

2 teaspoons orange-blossom water

1½ teaspoons vanilla extract

1 teaspoon finely grated orange zest

½ teaspoon ground cardamom

1 cup (2 sticks) unsalted butter, at room temperature

One 8-ounce package cream cheese, at room temperature

2 cups all-purpose flour, plus more for dusting

⅓ cup confectioners' sugar, plus more for dusting

Pinch of salt

1. In a small saucepan, combine the dates with ½ cup of the water. Simmer over low heat for 2 minutes, adding up to ¼ cup more water as necessary to achieve a

jamlike consistency. Pour the mixture onto a plate or a small baking sheet, and allow it to cool.

2. Combine the walnuts, honey, orange-blossom water, 1 teaspoon of the vanilla, the orange zest, and the cardamom in a small bowl, and mix well. Add the date mixture and stir until well combined. Set aside.

3. Combine the butter and cream cheese in the bowl of a standing mixer fitted with the paddle attachment and mix on low for 2 minutes, until smooth and creamy. Stop the machine and add the flour, confectioners' sugar, remaining ½ teaspoon vanilla, and salt. Mix on low for 2 minutes. Remove the dough, divide it in half, and press each into a flat disk. Wrap the disks in plastic wrap, and refrigerate for at least 2 hours and up to overnight.

4. Preheat the oven to 375°F.

5. Line two large baking sheets with parchment paper, or spray them with nonstick cooking spray.

6. On a lightly floured work surface, roll out 1 portion of the dough to a thickness of ⅛ inch. Using a 2½-inch round cookie cutter, cut out 12 rounds (you can reroll and cut any trimmings). Place them on the prepared baking sheets, and top each one with 1 to 1¼ teaspoons of the date-walnut filling.

7. Roll the second piece of dough to ⅛-inch thickness, and using a 3-inch round cookie cutter, cut out 12 rounds. Cover the filling with these larger rounds, and using the tines of a fork, press the edges of the cookies together. You can continue to reroll and cut dough trimmings and filling the cookies until you have used all the dough and filling.

8. Bake the cookies, one sheet at a time, until golden, 25 to 30 minutes, rotating the baking sheet halfway through. Set the baking sheets on wire racks and let the cookies cool on the sheets 2 minutes before transferring them to wire racks to cool completely.

9. Dust the cooled cookies generously with confectioners' sugar. The cookies can be stored in an airtight container at room temperature for up to 1 week or in the freezer for up to 1 month.

# CHOCOLATE WAFERS WITH PEANUT BUTTER FUDGE

18 sandwich cookies

Okay, we all know that chocolate and peanut butter make a perfect combination, so of course these sandwiches are a knockout. The best thing is that they're incredibly easy to make—and they also keep well.

### Chocolate wafers

1¾ cups all-purpose flour

½ cup unsweetened Dutch-process cocoa powder, sifted

1 teaspoon baking powder

12 tablespoons (1½ sticks) unsalted butter, at room temperature

¾ cup granulated sugar

1 large egg

2 teaspoons vanilla extract

### Peanut butter fudge

1½ cups creamy peanut butter

1½ cups marshmallow creme

⅓ cup confectioners' sugar

2 teaspoons vanilla extract

1. To make the chocolate wafers: In a medium mixing bowl, combine the flour, cocoa powder, and baking powder, and whisk to blend. Set aside.

2. In the bowl of a standing mixer fitted with the paddle attachment, combine the butter and granulated sugar, and blend well. Scrape down the sides of the bowl and then continue to mix until slightly fluffy. Add the egg and vanilla, and mix on medium speed until fully incorporated. Beat or stir in the flour mixture until incorporated.

3. Divide the dough in half and roll each half into a ball. Place each dough ball between two pieces of parchment or wax paper, and roll out to ⅛-inch thickness. Stack the rolled-out portions of dough on top of each other on a baking sheet, and refrigerate for at least 1 hour and up to overnight. (If it has been refrigerated overnight, allow the dough to warm up slightly at room temperature before cutting out the cookies.)

4. Line several baking sheets with parchment paper, or spray them with nonstick cooking spray.

5. Working with 1 piece of dough, peel away and discard 1 piece of the parchment paper. Using a 2¼-inch round cookie cutter, cut out 18 rounds (any dough trimmings can be rerolled and cut) and transfer them to one of the prepared baking sheets, spacing them 1 to 1½ inches apart. Repeat with the remaining dough. Refrigerate the cookies for 20 minutes before baking.

6. Meanwhile, preheat the oven to 350°F.

7. Bake the cookies for 6 minutes, or until they are almost firm. (Do not overbake the cookies or they will become too crisp.) Transfer the baking sheets to wire racks to cool for 2 to 3 minutes. Once the cookies have firmed up, transfer them to wire racks to cool completely.

8. To make the peanut butter fudge: Combine the peanut butter, marshmallow creme, confectioners' sugar, and the remaining 2 teaspoons vanilla in the bowl of a standing mixer fitted with the paddle attachment. Beat until the mixture begins to pull away from the sides of the bowl, forming a ball. Transfer the fudge to a sheet of parchment paper. Cover it with a second piece of parchment and press gently to flatten it. Using a rolling pin, roll the fudge out to a scant ¼-inch thickness. Transfer the fudge, still between the parchment, to a baking sheet and set it aside.

9. To assemble: Remove the top sheet of parchment paper, and using a 2¼-inch round cookie cutter, cut out 18 rounds of fudge. If necessary, reroll and cut any scraps. Place 1 piece of the fudge on half of the cookies. Place the remaining cookies on top, and gently sandwich together.

# PUMPKIN SPICE CAKES WITH PUMPKIN CREAM CENTERS

24 cakes

Pumpkin and spice are the ultimate signs of fall, conjuring up cozy thoughts of the holidays and wintry days ahead. These little cakes will warm up any party.

12 tablespoons (1½ sticks) unsalted butter, at room temperature

1 cup firmly packed light brown sugar

1 cup granulated sugar

3 large eggs

1 cup canned pumpkin puree (not pie filling)

½ cup buttermilk (see Note, page 64)

2 teaspoons vanilla extract

2 cups all-purpose flour

2 teaspoons baking powder

1½ teaspoons ground cinnamon

1 teaspoon baking soda

½ teaspoon freshly grated nutmeg

¼ teaspoon ground cloves

Pumpkin Cream (recipe follows)

Confectioners' sugar, for dusting

1. Preheat the oven to 350°F. Lightly coat two 12-cup standard muffin pans with cooking spray.

2. In the bowl of a standing mixer fitted with the paddle attachment, cream the butter and both sugars together until light and fluffy. Add the eggs one at a time, beating well after each addition.

3. In a separate medium mixing bowl, combine the pumpkin puree with the buttermilk and vanilla, and mix well. In another medium mixing bowl, combine the flour, baking powder, cinnamon, baking soda, nutmeg, and cloves, and mix well. In thirds, alternately add the flour mixture and the buttermilk mixture to the creamed butter, blending gently after each addition.

4. Using an ice cream scoop or a ¼-cup measure, scoop the batter into the prepared muffin cups. Bake until a toothpick inserted into the middle of a cake comes out clean, about 30 minutes. Cool the cakes in the pans on a wire rack for 15 minutes. Then remove the cakes from the pans and let them cool on the wire racks until completely cool.

5. To assemble: Slice each cake in half horizontally, and spoon 2 tablespoons of the Pumpkin Cream on the bottom half of each cake. Sandwich the cakes with the tops, and dust with confectioners' sugar.

## Pumpkin Cream

3 cups

1 cup whole milk

1¼ cups heavy cream

¾ cup granulated sugar

½ vanilla bean (about 3 inches), halved, seeds scraped out and reserved

⅛ teaspoon salt

¾ cup canned pumpkin puree (not pie filling)

¼ teaspoon pumpkin pie spice

4 large egg yolks

2½ tablespoons cornstarch

¼ cup confectioners' sugar

1 teaspoon ground cardamom

1 teaspoon vanilla extract

1. Combine the milk, ½ cup of the heavy cream, ½ cup of the granulated sugar, the vanilla bean and seeds, and the salt in a small saucepan. Whisk to combine, and bring to a boil over medium-high heat. Reduce the heat to a simmer and cook until the sugar has dissolved. Remove from the heat and discard the vanilla bean. Add the pumpkin puree and pumpkin pie spice, and whisk to combine.

2. In a separate bowl, combine the egg yolks, the remaining ¼ cup granulated sugar, and the cornstarch, and whisk well. Pour about 1 cup of the pumpkin mixture, ½ cup at a time, into the eggs and mix well. Pour the egg mixture into the pumpkin mixture, and return to the heat. Bring to a boil, stirring constantly with a heatproof rubber spatula. Immediately reduce the heat to low and continue to cook, stirring constantly, until the pudding thickens, 3 to 4 minutes. Remove from the heat and strain through a fine-mesh sieve or chinois into a clean bowl. Place plastic wrap directly on the surface of the pudding (so that the top does not develop a skin), and refrigerate until chilled, 2 hours or up to overnight.

3. In the bowl of a standing mixer fitted with the whisk attachment, combine the remaining ¾ cup heavy cream, the confectioners' sugar, the cardamom, and the vanilla. Beat on medium-high speed until soft peaks form, 2 to 3 minutes. Gently fold the whipped cream into the pumpkin cream. Keep refrigerated until ready to use.

Rustic Italian Bread,
see pages 286–289

# Knead
## BREAD?

# BRIOCHE BUNS OR LOAVES

8 buns or 2 loaves

The effort in making fresh bread yields its own reward. This rich, buttery brioche can be shaped and baked for a variety of uses—rolls, loaves, you name it. As a plus, any leftover bread is excellent for French toast. Be forewarned: your mixer will work hard and become extremely hot while kneading, but the long knead time is necessary to develop a fine, silky texture. Heavy-duty home mixers are designed to make bread dough; however, you must allow the machine to cool down completely once you finish mixing before using it again. If you have an older machine, you may want to stop your mixer at intervals during mixing to let it cool down a bit.

⅓ cup whole milk, warmed (no hotter than 110°F)

¼ cup sugar

1 packet active dry yeast (2¼ teaspoons)

4¼ cups all-purpose flour, plus more as needed

7 eggs

1½ teaspoons salt

1 cup (2 sticks) unsalted butter, cut into tablespoons,
    at room temperature

1 tablespoon water

1. Combine the milk, sugar, and yeast in the bowl of a standing mixer fitted with the dough hook. Let the mixture sit until it becomes foamy, about 5 minutes.

2. Add the flour, 4 of the eggs, and the salt to the milk mixture, and mix on low speed until combined. Add 2 more eggs, one at a time, mixing well after each

addition (save the remaining egg for making the egg wash). Raise the speed to medium-low and mix for 20 minutes, scraping the bowl and the hook about midway through. While the dough mixes, it will go through several stages, from wrapping completely around the hook, then falling, then wrapping around again. Allow the dough to mix for the full time.

3. Add the butter, a couple of tablespoons at a time, allowing it to become flattened and incorporated before adding more. This may take 5 to 10 minutes in all. During this stage the dough will fall apart and begin to make a slapping sound. In the end, the dough will come back together. Scrape the dough and the hook midway through. Once you have finished mixing, if the dough feels too sticky, add an additional 1 or 2 tablespoons of flour.

4. Transfer the dough to a lightly floured work surface, and knead it several times with floured hands to form it into a ball. Place the dough in a large bowl, cover it with plastic wrap, and set it aside in a warm, draft-free place until doubled in size, about 1½ hours.

5. Punch down the dough. Then transfer it to a large covered container or resealable plastic bag, and refrigerate it overnight.

### To make brioche rolls

1. Pull the chilled dough from the refrigerator and portion it into 8 equal pieces. Shape each portion into a roll by slightly cupping your hand over the dough and rolling the dough in a circular motion on the counter (if the dough is sticky, dust it with a little flour). After shaping them, place the rolls, seam side down, on a parchment-lined baking sheet. Cover them with plastic wrap or a kitchen towel, and let them rise in a warm, draft-free place until doubled. This may take 2 or more hours.

2. Preheat the oven to 375°F.

3. Use a fork to lightly beat the remaining egg with the water. Uncover the rolls and brush the egg wash all over them.

4. Place the baking sheet in the oven and bake the rolls for 5 minutes. Then rotate the sheet and reduce the heat to 350°F. Bake for 8 minutes longer, or until the rolls have risen, are golden brown, and register an internal temperature of 200°F when tested through the bottom with an instant-read thermometer. Remove from the oven and set aside to cool on the baking sheet.

5. Once they have cooled completely, the rolls can be wrapped in plastic wrap and stored overnight at room temperature, or frozen for up to 3 months.

### To make brioche loaves

1. Grease two 8½ x 4½-inch loaf pans with cooking spray. Divide the chilled dough in half. Roll on a lightly floured surface or stretch 1 piece of dough into a 12 x 5-inch rectangle. Fold one long side in one-third of the way, and press to seal. Fold the other side in one-third of the way, and press to seal. You should have a long, narrow rectangular piece of dough. Turn the shaped dough seam side down, fold the short ends under by 1 inch, and press to seal. Place the dough in a prepared loaf pan, seam side down. Repeat with the remaining dough. Cover the pans with a kitchen towel and set them aside in a warm, draft-free place until the dough has doubled in size, about 2 hours.

2. Preheat the oven to 375°F.

3. Use a fork to lightly beat the remaining egg with the water. Uncover the loaves and brush the egg wash all over them.

4. Place the loaf pans in the oven and bake for 10 minutes. Then rotate the pans and reduce the heat to 350°F. Bake for 15 minutes longer, or until the loaves have risen, are golden brown, and register an internal temperature of 200°F when tested through the bottom with an instant-read thermometer. Remove from the oven and let the loaves cool in the loaf pans for 10 minutes, then transfer the loaves to a wire rack.

5. Once they have cooled completely, the loaves can be wrapped in plastic wrap and stored overnight at room temperature, or frozen for up to 3 months.

## GREAT WITH

Breakfast Burger, page 234

Crab Louie Sandwich, page 155

New Orleans Shrimp Melt, page 164

Pork Tonkatsu with Pickled Vegetables, page 69

Portobello with Ricotta, Arugula, and Truffle Oil on Brioche, page 77

Mascarpone and Marmalade–Stuffed French Toast, page 226

Fried Soft-Shell Crab Sandwiches with Lemon Caper Mayo, page 8

Pistachio and Almond Gelato on Brioche Buns, page 260

# ENGLISH MUFFINS

8 English muffins

Making English muffins at home is not only easy but also really fun—it's a great Saturday morning activity with the kids. The muffins can be made in advance and kept well wrapped in the freezer for up to a month, so you can have homemade English muffins anytime.

1½ cups evaporated milk

1 tablespoon plus ¼ teaspoon sugar

1 teaspoon salt

1 tablespoon butter

1½ teaspoons active dry yeast

⅓ cup warm water (no hotter than 110°F)

2 cups all-purpose flour, sifted

½ teaspoon baking soda

1. In a small saucepan, combine the evaporated milk, 1 tablespoon sugar, the salt, and butter. Warm gently over low heat, stirring until the sugar and salt have completely dissolved. Pour the mixture into a medium bowl. If necessary, set aside until cooled to 110°F.

2. In a small bowl, combine the yeast, remaining ¼ teaspoon sugar, and the warm water, and set aside until the yeast is foamy, about 5 minutes.

3. Add the yeast mixture to the milk mixture. Add the flour and baking soda, and beat thoroughly with a wooden spoon until the flour is incorporated; it will be a sticky dough. Cover the bowl with plastic wrap and let the dough rest in a warm, draft-free spot for at least 30 minutes and up to 1 hour, until it has a thick consistency with visible bubbles.

4. Preheat a cast-iron griddle or a large skillet over medium heat.

5. Lightly coat four 3-inch English muffin rings (see Note) with cooking spray, and place them on the griddle. Using a measuring cup or an ice cream scoop, portion ¼ to ⅓ cup of the dough into each ring. Cover the rings with a baking sheet and cook for 5 minutes, or until the bottoms begin to brown. Remove the baking sheet and use tongs to flip the rings over. Replace the baking sheet and cook for another 5 minutes, or until golden brown. Transfer the muffins, in their rings, to a wire rack; then remove the rings. Repeat, using clean rings, until all of the dough has been used.

6. Serve immediately, or store in an airtight container in the freezer for up to 1 month.

Note: If you do not have English muffin rings, you can substitute metal cookie cutters (without handles) or tuna cans that have both the tops and bottoms removed and have been cleaned and sanitized.

## GREAT WITH

Poached Eggs with Prosciutto-Wrapped Asparagus and Béarnaise Sauce, page 232

Herbed Goat Cheese and Egg on an English Muffin, page 224

# HERBED FOCACCIA

10 to 12 servings

If you have a bit of leftover mashed potato, this is what you do with it: make tender, delicious bread. Though you already know there's nothing like fresh bread, this recipe will show you why focaccia is a favorite.

2 tablespoons olive oil

2 cups chopped onion (see Note)

1½ cups warm water (no hotter than 110°F)

1½ teaspoons sugar

1 packet active dry yeast (2¼ teaspoons)

5 cups all-purpose flour, plus more as needed

1¼ cups chopped mixed fresh herb leaves,
    such as basil, rosemary, oregano, thyme, and parsley

½ cup mashed cooked potato

½ cup plus 3 tablespoons extra-virgin olive oil,
    plus more for greasing

1¾ teaspoons salt

Cornmeal, for dusting

½ teaspoon kosher salt or other coarse salt

1. Heat the olive oil in a small sauté pan over medium-high heat. Add the onion and cook until it is softened and light in color, about 5 minutes. Remove from the heat and set aside to cool.

2. Combine the warm water, sugar, and yeast in the bowl of a standing mixer fitted with the dough hook. Let the mixture sit until it becomes foamy, about 5 minutes.

3. Add the flour, half of the herbs, the mashed potato, the 3 tablespoons extra-virgin olive oil, and the salt to the yeast mixture. Mix on low speed for 10 minutes, scraping the dough and the hook about halfway through. The dough will come together and begin to pull away from the bowl. (Alternatively, you can mix the dough with a wooden spoon in a wide shallow bowl. Once you stir everything together, transfer the dough to a lightly floured work surface, and knead until smooth, about 10 minutes.)

4. Transfer the dough to a lightly floured work surface and knead it several times with floured hands to form it into a ball. Put the dough in a lightly oiled large mixing bowl, turn the dough so the entire surface is lightly oiled, cover the bowl with plastic wrap, and set it aside in a warm, draft-free place until the dough has doubled in size, about 1 hour. Punch down the dough, recover the bowl, and set it aside again to rise a second time, until doubled in size, about 1 hour.

5. Line an 11¾ x 7½-inch rimmed baking sheet or a jelly roll pan with parchment paper, and dust it with cornmeal.

6. Transfer the dough to a lightly floured work surface and knead it several times with lightly floured hands to form it into a ball. Lightly dust a rolling pin with flour, and roll the dough out to form a 12 x 16-inch rectangle; you may also use your hands to stretch the dough to manipulate it into the shape of the baking sheet. It will be pliable, yet want to shrink. Transfer the dough to the prepared baking sheet and set it aside, covered, to rise a final time, about 1 hour.

7. Preheat the oven to 450°F.

8. Combine the remaining herbs with the remaining ½ cup extra-virgin olive oil in a small bowl.

9. Gently dimple the dough all over with your fingertips, leaving indentations about ½ inch deep. Brush the dough all over with half of the herb oil. Sprinkle the kosher salt over the top. Bake for 10 minutes. Then rotate the baking sheet from back to front, and bake for 6 minutes longer, until golden. Remove the focaccia from the oven and brush it with the remaining herb oil. Serve hot or at room temperature.

Note: You can use a variety of flavorings for focaccia. Instead of onion and herbs (or along with them) you can use olives, cheese, pesto, sun-dried tomatoes, and so on. You can always adjust the wetness of the dough (depending on its flavoring) by adding more flour as needed.

## GREAT WITH

Sandwich Caprese, page 169

Sandwich Niçoise, page 19

Egg Salad Supreme, page 33

Olive Oil–Poached Tuna Salad Sandwich with Citrus Aïoli, page 34

# HONEY WHOLE WHEAT BREAD

Two 1¾-pound loaves

This loaf contains less wheat than some heartier varieties. It's still a wholesome bread, and the great news is that my kids love it, so yours will too. The honey adds just a touch of sweetness but also makes the bread tender and light. Rest assured, this loaf provides the best of both worlds.

2¼ cups whole milk, warmed
   (no hotter than 110°F)
1 packet active dry yeast
   (2¼ teaspoons)
¼ cup honey
4 cups bread flour or all-purpose flour
2½ cups whole wheat flour
1 tablespoon unsalted butter, at room temperature,
   plus more for greasing
1 tablespoon unsulphured molasses
1 tablespoon kosher salt

1. Pour ½ cup of the warm milk into the bowl of a standing mixer fitted with the dough hook. Add the yeast and honey, and whisk to blend. Allow the mixture to rest until the yeast looks creamy and there are a few bubbles, about 5 minutes.

2. In a separate large bowl, combine 3½ cups of the bread flour with all the whole wheat flour.

3. Add the remaining 1¾ cups warm milk, the butter, the molasses, and about half of the flour mixture to the bowl of the standing mixer. Start the mixer on low speed and begin mixing the dough. If flour begins to fly out of the bowl, turn the mixer

on and off a few times to just combine the flour. Every so often, stop the machine and scrape down the bowl and the hook. Once the dough comes together, add the salt, increase the mixer speed to medium, and knead the dough for about 10 minutes, or until it becomes smooth and elastic. If the mixer begins to get warm, you can remove the dough and knead it by hand on a lightly floured work surface. Kneading by hand allows you to get a feel for the dough.

4. Shape the dough into a ball and place it in a lightly oiled or buttered large bowl. Turn the dough in the bowl so the entire surface is lightly oiled. Cover the bowl with plastic wrap or a kitchen towel, and place it in a warm, draft-free place for at least 1½ hours, or until the dough has doubled in bulk.

5. Butter two 8½ x 4½-inch loaf pans and set them aside. Punch the dough down and turn it out onto a lightly floured work surface. Divide the dough in half. Using your hands or a rolling pin, shape each piece of dough into a flat rectangle. To form each loaf, beginning at the top of the rectangle (the longer side facing you), fold down the top third of the dough, and press gently along the seam with your fingertips to seal it. Fold down again and seal. Place the loaves, seam down, in the buttered pans.

6. Loosely cover the pans with a sheet of oiled plastic wrap, and allow the dough to rise in a warm, draft-free place until doubled in size, about 1 hour.

7. Position an oven rack in the center of the oven and preheat the oven to 375°F.

8. Use a sharp knife to slash the top of each loaf decoratively, if desired, and place the pans in the oven. Bake for 35 minutes, or until the loaves are golden brown and the internal temperature registers 200°F on an instant-read thermometer. Remove the loaves from their pans and let them cool on wire racks. Do not slice the bread until it is completely cool.

9. The bread can be kept in a brown paper bag wrapped in plastic wrap for 2 to 3 days. For longer storage, wrap it in plastic wrap and then in aluminum foil and store it in the freezer for up to 1 month.

## GREAT WITH

Grilled Peanut Butter, Banana, and Honey, page 136

Grilled Idiazábal Cheese with Quince Paste, Pears, and Walnut Butter, page 131

Quadrello di Bufala with Pan-Crisped Prosciutto, Honeyed Figs, and Frisée, page 172

Lyonnaise Sandwich, page 223

# RUSTIC ITALIAN BREAD

2 loaves

This is the perfect bread to make any time you're looking for a crusty seeded loaf. Use it in place of muffuletta bread for that iconic New Orleans favorite, if you like. Or enjoy it on its own, warm from the oven— slather it with butter or dip it in olive oil and you're there.

2¼ cups warm water (no hotter than 110°F)

1 packet plus 1 teaspoon active dry yeast (3¼ teaspoons)

5¾ cups bread flour, plus more for dusting

2 tablespoons dark brown sugar

2 tablespoons extra-virgin olive oil, plus more for greasing

1 tablespoon plus ½ teaspoon salt

Cornmeal, for dusting

1 egg white, lightly beaten

1 tablespoon sesame seeds

1. Combine the warm water and the yeast in the bowl of a standing mixer fitted with the dough hook. Let the mixture sit until it becomes foamy, about 5 minutes.

2. Add the flour and brown sugar to the yeast mixture, and mix on low speed until the dough starts to form. Drizzle in the oil and salt, and beat on medium speed for 8 to 10 minutes, or until a smooth, firm, elastic dough is formed.

3. Lightly oil the inside of a large mixing bowl. The dough will be sticky; dusting your hands with flour will make handling easier. Use a spatula lightly dusted with flour (or a bowl scraper) to remove the dough from the hook and transfer it to the oiled mixing bowl. Turn the dough so the entire surface is lightly oiled, cover the

bowl with plastic wrap, and set it aside in a warm, draft-free place until the dough has doubled in size, about 1½ hours.

4. Transfer the dough to a lightly floured work surface. Cut the dough in half, and punch each half down by pressing it with the heel of your hand into a flat rectangular shape. To form each loaf, beginning at the top of the rectangle (the longer side facing you), fold down the top third of the dough, and press gently along the seam with your fingertips to seal it. Fold down again and seal.

5. Generously dust two baker's peels or inverted baking sheets with cornmeal, and place a loaf on each one. Loosely cover the loaves with a damp towel, and let them rise in a warm, draft-free spot until doubled in size, 1 to 2 hours.

6. Place a baking stone in the lower third of the oven, and preheat the oven to 425°F. (Alternatively, an inverted baking sheet may be used in place of a baking stone.)

7. Brush the loaves with the egg white and sprinkle the sesame seeds over the top. Using a razor blade or a sharp knife, score three ¼-inch-deep slashes across the top of each loaf at a 45-degree angle.

8. Before baking each loaf, spray it generously with water from a spray bottle (if you don't have a spray bottle, dip a basting brush in water and generously sprinkle it over the dough). Then slide the dough onto the baking stone, immediately close the oven door, and bake for 3 minutes. Open the oven door and spray the dough again. Close the oven door and bake for an additional 3 minutes before spraying the dough for a third time (the spraying of the dough will ensure a crisp, golden brown crust). Bake the dough for 25 to 30 minutes, or until an instant-read thermometer inserted into the bottom of the bread registers 200°F. Place the bread on a cooling rack and let it sit for at least 10 minutes before slicing. Repeat with the remaining loaf.

## GREAT WITH

Grilled Truffled Cheese Sandwiches with
Prosciutto and Mushrooms, page 134

Spicy Eggplant with Mozzarella and Basil, page 143

Eggplant Muffuletta, page 27

Artichoke, Salami, and Fontina Panini, page 145

Porchetta with Dandelion Greens, page 161

# PITA BREAD

16 pitas

Pita is one of the most versatile breads I can think of. The bread can be made with all white flour, all whole wheat flour, or a combination of the two. Pita is a flatbread, but when the dough hits the hot stone or baking sheet it will puff up, forming a pocket. Pitas can be either filled or folded, and the leftovers, if there are any, are perfect for making pita chips.

1 packet active dry yeast (2¼ teaspoons)
2½ cups lukewarm water (no hotter than 110°F)
3 to 3½ cups whole wheat flour
2½ to 3 cups unbleached all-purpose flour
1 tablespoon sea salt
2 tablespoons olive oil

1. In a large mixing bowl, combine the yeast and warm water, and stir to dissolve the yeast. In a separate bowl, combine the two flours. Using a wooden spoon, stir about half of the flour into the yeast mixture and continue to stir for 1½ minutes, always moving the spoon in the same direction. This will activate the gluten, and the dough will look like a batter or a sponge. Allow the sponge to rest, covered, in a warm, draft-free place for at least 30 minutes and up to 2 hours.

2. Sprinkle the salt over the top of the sponge and stir in the olive oil. Add the remaining flour, 1 cup at a time, and mix well. As soon as the dough becomes too stiff to stir, turn it out onto a lightly floured surface and knead it for 8 to 10 minutes. (Alternatively, you can knead it in a standing mixer using the dough hook.) The dough should look smooth and elastic. Place the dough in a lightly oiled bowl and turn it so that all sides are lightly covered in oil. Cover the bowl with plastic wrap and place it in a warm, draft-free place until the dough has doubled in size, about 1½ hours.

3. Punch down the dough and divide it into 2 balls. (At this point, the dough can be stored in a large resealable plastic bag in the refrigerator for up to 1 week. When you want to use it, simply cut off the amount of dough you need and keep the remaining dough in the refrigerator. The dough develops more flavor the longer it sits. Allow the dough to come to room temperature before proceeding.) Cover the dough with a damp kitchen towel to keep it from drying out.

4. Line the oven with quarry tiles or place a large baking stone (or two baking sheets) in the bottom third of the oven. Preheat the oven to 450°F.

5. Lightly flour your hands, a work surface, and a rolling pin. Divide one of the balls of dough into 8 equal pieces and flatten each. Working one at a time (keeping the remaining pieces covered with a damp kitchen towel), roll into an 8-inch round about ¼ inch thick. Cover it, and repeat with the remaining pieces. Do not stack the rounds, or they may stick to one another.

6. Place as many rolled-out rounds as will fit in the oven, and bake for 3 to 5 minutes, until the breads have puffed up. (The breads should begin to puff up in the first minute. Don't worry if the pitas do not puff up all over or puff only slightly; they will still taste great.) As soon as the breads come out of the oven, wrap them in a kitchen towel to keep them from drying out. Repeat as desired.

7. Once the bread is baked, it should be wrapped in a resealable plastic bag, but pita bread is best if eaten the day it is baked.

## GREAT WITH

Falafel with Cucumber, Onion, and Tomato Salad, page 176

Beef Shawarma with Tzatziki Sauce, page 179

Orange and Herb–Roasted Lamb Pita, page 207

Smashed Chickpeas on Naan with Cilantro-Mint Chutney, page 170

White Bean Hummus with Roasted Veggies on Lavash, page 40

# POTATO ROLLS

8 rolls

These slightly sweet and pillowy rolls are perfect for the dinner table and also make for a delicious sandwich. I love using them to make the pork bun sandwich on page 69, but they're just right any time you're looking for a soft, tender crumb.

¼ cup whole milk, warmed (no hotter than 110°F)

¼ cup sugar

1 packet active dry yeast (2¼ teaspoons)

Vegetable oil, for greasing

2½ cups all-purpose flour, plus more for dusting

1½ tablespoons kosher salt

4 tablespoons (½ stick) butter, melted

2 large eggs, lightly whisked, plus 1 whole egg

1¼ cups mashed or riced cooked Idaho or russet potato

2 tablespoons heavy cream

1. Combine the warm milk, 1 tablespoon of the sugar, and the yeast in a large mixing bowl and set aside until foamy, 5 to 10 minutes.

2. Lightly oil the inside of another large mixing bowl, and set it aside.

3. Add the flour, remaining 3 tablespoons sugar, salt, butter, and the 2 whisked eggs to the yeast mixture, and using a wooden spoon, stir to blend well. When the dough begins to clump, add the potato and stir together until the dough forms a mass. Transfer the dough to a lightly floured work surface and knead until it comes together and is smooth and springy, 2 to 3 minutes (dust your hands and work surface with flour for easier handling). Then transfer the dough to the oiled bowl.

Turn the dough so the entire surface is lightly oiled, cover the bowl with plastic wrap, and let it sit in a warm, draft-free place until the dough has doubled in size and small bubbles appear on the surface, about 1½ hours.

4. Lightly grease a baking sheet with oil.

5. Transfer the dough to a lightly floured work surface; the dough will be sticky, so dust your hands as necessary to ease handling. Punch down the dough and then knead it several times to form a ball. Using a dough scraper or a knife, divide the dough into 8 equal portions. Shape each portion into a roll by slightly cupping your hand over the dough and rolling the dough in a circular motion on the counter (if the dough is sticky, dust it with a little flour). After shaping them, place the rolls, seam side down, on the prepared baking sheet; stagger the rolls, leaving about 2 inches of space in between. Lightly brush the rolls with oil. Cover the rolls loosely with plastic wrap and let them rise in a warm, draft-free spot until doubled in size, about 1 hour.

6. Preheat the oven to 375°F.

7. In a small bowl, whisk together the remaining egg and the heavy cream. Brush the rolls with the egg mixture, and transfer the baking sheet to the oven. Bake until the rolls are golden brown and the internal temperature registers 200°F when tested with an instant-read thermometer, 20 to 25 minutes. Remove from the oven and set on a wire rack to cool.

8. The cooled bread can be wrapped in plastic wrap and stored overnight at room temperature or frozen for up to 3 months.

## GREAT WITH

Seared Salmon with Gingered Radish Pickle and Soy Mayo on a Roll, page 73

Pork Tonkatsu with Pickled Vegetables, page 69

BBQ Pork Ribs, Chinese Style, page 59

# PUMPERNICKEL

I round loaf

You have got to try this wonderful rich dark bread. Blackstrap molasses, unsweetened chocolate, and a bit of espresso powder lend gorgeous color as well as intensely delicious, complex flavor. Make a fantastic Reuben with this one, or simply pair it with smoked salmon. I also love it with the Curried Chicken Salad on Pumpernickel on page 51.

¾ cup water

¼ cup blackstrap molasses (see Note)

2 tablespoons whole milk

2 tablespoons unsalted butter

1 tablespoon caraway seeds

2 teaspoons salt

1½ teaspoons instant espresso powder

1 teaspoon fennel seeds, ground

¼ cup yellow cornmeal

1 ounce unsweetened chocolate

¼ cup warm water (no hotter than 110°F)

1 packet active dry yeast (2¼ teaspoons)

2 teaspoons sugar

1½ cups rye flour (preferably dark rye flour)

1½ cups bread flour

¼ cup whole wheat flour

Vegetable oil, for greasing

1. Combine the water, molasses, milk, butter, caraway seeds, salt, espresso powder, and ground fennel seeds in a small pot and bring to a boil over medium heat. Whisk in the cornmeal and remove the pot from the heat. Add the chocolate and stir until melted. Allow the mixture to cool until tepid, about 10 minutes.

2. Combine the warm water, yeast, and sugar in the bowl of a standing mixer fitted with the dough hook. Let the mixture sit until it becomes bubbly or creamy, about 5 minutes. Add the three flours and the cornmeal mixture. Mix on low speed until combined. Continue to mix for 10 minutes, scraping the hook about halfway through.

3. Transfer the dough to a lightly floured work surface, knead it several times with lightly floured hands, and form it into a ball. Lightly oil a medium mixing bowl, and add the dough, turning it once to oil the top. Cover the bowl with a kitchen towel and set it in a warm, draft-free place until the dough has increased by half, 2 to 3 hours.

4. Remove the dough from the bowl, knead it several times with lightly floured hands, and form it into a ball. Set it on a parchment-lined baking sheet, cover it with a kitchen towel, and set it aside to rise a second time, 1 to 1½ hours. Once it has increased by half, the dough is ready to bake.

5. Position an oven rack in the top third of the oven, and preheat the oven to 350°F. Fill a small spray bottle with water.

6. Right before baking, use a serrated knife to slash an X in the top of the dough. Spray water all over the dough. Bake for 1 hour and 5 minutes, spraying the dough several times during the first 10 minutes, and rotating the baking sheet halfway through baking. The bread is done when it registers an internal temperature of 200°F on an instant-read thermometer inserted through the bottom. Transfer the bread to a wire rack to cool.

7. The cooled bread can be wrapped in plastic wrap and stored overnight at room temperature or frozen for up to 3 months.

Note: Blackstrap molasses is a dark, less sweet, but strong-flavored molasses. If you need a substitute, try barley malt syrup or robust molasses. Though there may be a slight difference in color and flavor, the bread will still be delicious.

## GREAT WITH

Pork Rillette on Pumpernickel with
Watercress and Fig Vinaigrette, page 151

The Reuben, page 3

The Rachel, page 4

Curried Chicken Salad on Pumpernickel, page 51

Grilled Idiazábal Cheese with Quince Paste,
Pears, and Walnut Butter, page 131

# SEMOLINA PIZZA DOUGH

Two 12- or 14-inch pizzas, or 4 calzones

Use this simple pizza dough any time you want to make pizzas or calzones.
I promise you won't be disappointed.

1½ cups warm water (about 110°F)

1 packet active dry yeast (2¼ teaspoons)

1 teaspoon sugar

½ cup olive oil, plus more for greasing

½ cup semolina flour

3½ cups unbleached all-purpose flour, plus more for dusting

1¼ teaspoons salt

1. Combine the warm water, yeast, and sugar in the bowl of a standing mixer fitted with the dough hook. Let the mixture sit until it begins to look creamy or bubbly, about 5 minutes.

2. Add the olive oil, semolina, all-purpose flour, and salt to the yeast mixture, and mix on medium speed for 10 minutes, until the dough is smooth, scraping the dough hook midway. Transfer the dough to a lightly floured work surface, and knead it two to three times with floured hands to form it into a ball.

3. Oil a large mixing bowl, add the dough, turn to coat with oil, and cover it with plastic wrap. Set the bowl aside in a warm, draft-free place until the dough has doubled in size, about 1 hour.

4. Punch down the dough, and allow it to rise a second time until it has doubled in size, about 1 hour.

5. Divide the dough into two 8-ounce pieces, shape them into balls, and let them rest for about 15 minutes before rolling them out.

Note: If you make this dough way ahead of time, divide it into 8-ounce pieces after the first rise, roll them into balls, cover, and refrigerate until ready to use (up to overnight). The dough can also be frozen for up to 3 months (just thaw it in the refrigerator for several hours before using). Be sure to let the dough sit out at room temperature for 20 minutes or so before rolling it out.

## GREAT WITH

Sopressata and Genoa Salami Calzones, page 181

# TWO-DAY MULTIGRAIN

I loaf

If you like hearty breads chock-full of seeds, nuts, and whole grains, then this one is for you! It takes two days to make but it's so simple—you hardly have to do a thing. Mix, rest, bake! It's perfect for breakfast, because it will keep you feeling satisfied all morning long, and it's a great base for an open-face sandwich. Don't fret about the lengthy ingredient list: most of the flours, seeds, and nuts are easy to find in the bulk foods aisle of your local Whole Foods or gourmet market.

2 cups unbleached bread flour, plus more for dusting

1 cup whole wheat flour

½ cup oat flour

½ cup buckwheat or barley flour

2 tablespoons raw sunflower seeds or pumpkin seeds

2 tablespoons flax seeds

2 tablespoons poppy seeds

1 tablespoon sesame seeds

2 tablespoons raw wheat germ

2 teaspoons kosher salt

1 packet active dry yeast (2¼ teaspoons)

2 cups warm water (no hotter than 110°F)

2 tablespoons honey or agave nectar

2 tablespoons whole milk or soy milk

Blue cornmeal, for dusting

1. In a large bowl, combine the four flours, four types of seeds, wheat germ, salt, and yeast. Mix well. Add the water, honey, and milk, and stir thoroughly to combine. Cover the bowl with plastic wrap and set it aside in a warm, draft-free place for at least 18 hours and up to 24 hours—until it has nearly doubled in size and is dotted with bubbles.

2. Remove the plastic wrap and dust the top of the dough with a little bread flour, evenly distributing it across the top. Using a bowl scraper, scrape the dough down along the sides of the bowl to form a ball. Cover the bowl with plastic wrap and set it aside in a warm, draft-free place until slightly risen, 3 to 4 hours.

3. Preheat the oven to 450°F.

4. Place a Dutch oven on a rack in the bottom third of the oven, and preheat it for 30 minutes. Using oven mitts, remove the Dutch oven, and reduce the oven temperature to 425°F. Scatter the blue cornmeal over the bottom of the Dutch oven, and pour the dough into the pan. Cover the Dutch oven with the lid and return it to the oven.

5. Bake for 30 minutes. Then remove the lid and bake for another 20 minutes or until the bread is browned and crusty and has pulled away from the sides of the pan. Remove the Dutch oven and turn the loaf out onto a wire rack. Let it cool completely before slicing.

6. The cooled bread can be wrapped in plastic wrap and stored overnight at room temperature or frozen for up to 3 months.

## GREAT WITH

Three-Cheese Veggie Sandwich, page 36

Turkey Waldorf Sandwich, page 21

# WHITE SANDWICH BREAD

2 loaves

Here's a recipe for the quintessential soft, tender, full-flavored white sandwich loaf. These loaves are easily made midmorning to be enjoyed by early afternoon. They take little kneading . . . well, relatively speaking. It *is* homemade bread, for goodness' sake!

2 large eggs

2½ cups whole milk

6 tablespoons (¾ stick) unsalted butter

3 tablespoons sugar

2 packets active dry yeast (4½ teaspoons)

8 cups bread flour

2½ teaspoons salt

Oil or melted butter, for greasing

1. Put the eggs in a large mixing bowl.

2. Heat the milk and 4 tablespoons of the butter in a liquid measure in the microwave, or in a small pot on the stove, until the milk is warmed and the butter is melted. Remove from the heat, and if necessary set aside until cooled to no warmer than 110°F.

3. Add the milk mixture and the sugar to the eggs, and whisk to combine. Stir in the yeast and let the mixture sit until it is foamy, about 5 minutes.

4. Add 7 cups of the flour, and then the salt, to the yeast mixture. Using a wooden spoon, stir until incorporated. Add another ½ cup flour and begin kneading it into the dough with your hands by pulling the dough toward you in the bowl

and pressing down. Continue in this manner until the flour is incorporated, about 5 minutes. If the dough isn't pulling completely away from the bowl and is still sticking to the sides, knead in the remaining ½ cup of flour. Transfer the dough to a floured work surface and form it into a ball.

5. Drizzle a bit of oil or melted butter in the same bowl and add the dough, turning it once to grease the top. Cover the bowl with a kitchen towel and set it in a warm, draft-free place until the dough has increased by half (not doubled), 1 to 1½ hours.

6. Grease two 8½ x 4½-inch loaf pans with the remaining 2 tablespoons butter.

7. Transfer the dough to a lightly floured work surface and knead it several times. Divide the dough in half. Roll or stretch 1 portion of the dough into a 12 x 5-inch rectangle. Fold one long side in one third of the way, and press to seal it. Fold the other side one third of the way lengthwise and press to seal. Turn the shaped dough, seam side down, fold the ends under by 1 inch, and press to seal. Place the dough in the prepared loaf pan, seam side down. Repeat with the remaining dough. Cover the loaves with a kitchen towel and return them to the warm, draft-free place. Allow them to rise until doubled in size, 1 to 1½ hours.

8. Preheat the oven to 350°F.

9. Bake the loaves in the oven for 40 minutes, or until the tops are golden and the internal temperature reads 200°F when tested through the bottom with an instant-read thermometer. Transfer the loaves to wire racks and allow them to cool for at least 30 minutes before slicing.

## GREAT WITH

Smoky Grilled Pimento Cheese, page 126

Grilled Spinach and Artichoke Dip Sandwich, page 141

Egg Salad Supreme, page 33

BLT with Fried Green Tomatoes and Shrimp Rémoulade, page 5

Emeril's Monte Cristo, page 15

Heirloom Tomato Sandwich, page 25

# DRESS
# IT UP

Homemade
Mayonnaise

Green
Peppercorn
Mayo

Soy Mayo

Jalapeño
Mayo

Citrus Aïoli

Herbed Aïoli

Spicy Sesame
Mayo

Lemon Caper Mayo

Kalamata Olive
Mayo

Creole Mustard Mayo

# MAYOS AND AÏOLIS

## HOMEMADE MAYONNAISE

**1½ cups**

Once you've perfected this simple classic, you'll hesitate about going back to store-bought. My version here has a hint of garlic, but if you're not a garlic lover, simply omit it and the mayonnaise will be just as delicious.

1 large egg, at room temperature (see box)

1 large egg yolk, at room temperature

1½ teaspoons freshly squeezed lemon juice, or more to taste

½ teaspoon Dijon mustard

½ to ¾ teaspoon minced garlic

½ teaspoon kosher salt, or more to taste

¼ teaspoon freshly ground white pepper or ground cayenne pepper, or more to taste

1 cup vegetable oil

¼ cup olive oil

In the bowl of a food processor, combine the egg, egg yolk, lemon juice, mustard, garlic, salt, and pepper. Process on high speed until smooth, light yellow, and frothy, about 1 minute. While the processor is still running, combine the vegetable and olive oils in a measuring cup with a pour spout, and working very slowly, add the oil to the processor in a thin, steady stream, processing until the oil is completely incorporated and a thick emulsion is formed. (It is very important that the oil is added very slowly, especially at the beginning, otherwise the mayonnaise may break.) Transfer the mayonnaise to a nonreactive bowl, and add more salt, pepper, and/or lemon juice if desired. Use immediately, or refrigerate in an airtight nonreactive container for up to 3 days.

RAW EGG WARNING: I suggest using caution when consuming raw eggs because of the slight risk of salmonella or other food-borne illness. To reduce this risk, I recommend that you use only fresh, properly refrigerated, clean, grade A or AA eggs with intact shells, and always avoid contact between the yolks or whites and the outside portion of the eggshell.

# CREOLE MUSTARD MAYO

About 1½ cups

This Creole mustard and mayonnaise mix makes for a perfect all-purpose sandwich spread. I particularly love it on sandwiches with roasted meats. If you can't find Creole mustard in your area, substitute a hearty whole-grain or crushed-grain spicy mustard in its place, or make your own Creole mustard.

¾ cup mayonnaise, preferably homemade (see page 309)

½ cup plus 1 tablespoon sour cream

¼ cup plus 2 tablespoons Creole mustard (see page 318) or whole-grain mustard

¾ teaspoon cayenne pepper

Place the mayonnaise, sour cream, mustard, and cayenne in a small mixing bowl and stir together until combined. Use immediately, or cover with plastic wrap and store in the refrigerator until ready to use, up to 3 days.

# GREEN PEPPERCORN MAYO

1 generous cup

This assertive mayonnaise adds quite a kick to burgers such as the Blue Cheese–Stuffed Skillet Burger with Green Peppercorn Mayo (page 81).

1 egg yolk (see box, page 309), at room temperature

2 tablespoons white wine vinegar

2 teaspoons Dijon mustard

1 tablespoon plus 1 teaspoon green peppercorns, drained

1 cup vegetable oil

½ teaspoon salt

In the bowl of a food processor, combine the egg yolk, vinegar, mustard, and peppercorns. Process for 30 seconds. While the machine is still running, slowly add the oil through the feed tube to form an emulsion. Add the salt. Use immediately, or transfer the mayonnaise to a container, cover, and refrigerate for up to 3 days.

# JALAPEÑO MAYO

**1½ cups**

Keep this in the fridge to wake up your old standby roast beef or turkey and cheese sandwich, or use it with fried seafood, such as the oyster po'boy on page 95.

1 large egg (see box, page 309), at room temperature

1 large egg yolk, at room temperature

2 tablespoons chopped fresh cilantro leaves (optional)

1 tablespoon freshly squeezed lemon juice

1 teaspoon minced garlic

½ teaspoon Dijon mustard

2 to 3 jalapeños, stemmed, seeded, and chopped

1 cup vegetable oil

¾ teaspoon salt

Freshly ground black pepper or cayenne pepper, to taste

In a food processor or a blender, combine the egg, egg yolk, cilantro (if using), lemon juice, garlic, mustard, and jalapeños, and process until smooth. With the motor still running, add the oil in a thin stream until a thick emulsion is formed. Add the salt and pepper, and transfer the mayonnaise to a nonreactive container. Use immediately, or cover and refrigerate for up to 3 days.

# KALAMATA OLIVE MAYO

**About 1 cup**

This would be delicious on the Heirloom Tomato Sandwich on page 25. It's also a terrific addition to something as simple as boiled new potatoes: Cook the potatoes until just tender, then toss them with some of the Kalamata Olive Mayo and some chopped fresh herbs. As the potatoes cool, they'll soak up the intense flavors.

1 large egg yolk (see box, page 309), at room temperature

Finely grated zest of 1 lemon (about ½ teaspoon)

1 teaspoon freshly squeezed lemon juice

1 tablespoon Dijon mustard

½ cup canola, grapeseed, or other neutral-flavored oil

¼ cup extra-virgin olive oil

½ cup chopped pitted Kalamata olives

Combine the egg yolk, lemon zest, lemon juice, and Dijon mustard in a small bowl. Slowly drizzle in the oils while whisking vigorously to form an emulsion. Stir in the olives. Use immediately, or cover and refrigerate for up to 3 days.

## LEMON CAPER MAYO

### 1⅓ cups

Slide the ketchup aside—this is the secret side to fantastic French fries. I'm not kidding. Dip 'em and see for yourself.

1 large egg (see box, page 309), at room temperature

1 tablespoon minced garlic

3 tablespoons freshly squeezed lemon juice

1 tablespoon Creole mustard (see page 318) or whole-grain mustard

1 teaspoon salt

¼ teaspoon cayenne pepper

1 cup olive oil

1 tablespoon chopped fresh parsley leaves

2 tablespoons capers, drained, rinsed, and chopped

1.  Put the egg, garlic, lemon juice, mustard, salt, and cayenne in the bowl of a food processor and puree for 15 seconds. With the processor running, add the oil through the feed tube in a slow, steady stream, blending until the mayonnaise becomes thick. Transfer the mayonnaise to a bowl and fold in the parsley and capers.

2.  Cover and refrigerate until well chilled before serving, about 1 hour. The mayonnaise can be stored in an airtight container in the refrigerator for up to 3 days.

# SOY MAYO

About ¾ cup

You'll have a hard time keeping your fingers out of the soy glaze that's the basis of this flavored mayo. It's truly versatile—any leftover reduced soy glaze can be kept indefinitely at room temperature and used to drizzle on grilled salmon or tuna.

¼ cup sugar

¼ cup soy sauce

¾ cup mayonnaise, homemade (see page 309), or store-bought

1. Combine the sugar and soy sauce in a very small saucepan and cook over medium-low heat until reduced to a syrup, about 5 minutes. The soy-sugar mixture should coat the back of a spoon. Set it aside to cool completely.

2. Stir 2 tablespoons of the soy glaze into the mayonnaise. Use immediately or refrigerate for up to 3 days until ready to use.

# SPICY SESAME MAYO

1½ cups

I serve this mayo with the Teriyaki-Glazed Pork Tenderloin Sandwiches (page 38), but it would also be awesome with the Spicy Tuna Poke on page 148 and the Fresh Tuna and Butter Lettuce Wraps on page 194.

1 large egg (see box, page 309), at room temperature

1 large egg yolk, at room temperature

1 tablespoon Sriracha sauce

1½ teaspoons freshly squeezed lime juice

½ teaspoon Dijon mustard

¾ teaspoon minced garlic

½ teaspoon kosher salt

¼ teaspoon cayenne pepper

1 cup vegetable or peanut oil

¼ cup hot sesame oil

In the bowl of a food processor, combine the egg, egg yolk, Sriracha sauce, lime juice, Dijon mustard, garlic, salt, and cayenne. Process until smooth, about 1 minute. While the processor is still running, combine the vegetable and sesame oils in a liquid measuring cup with a spout, and working very slowly, add the oil to the processor in a thin, steady stream, processing until the oil is completely incorporated and a thick emulsion is formed. Use immediately or store, covered, in the refrigerator for up to 3 days.

## CITRUS AÏOLI

About ⅔ cup

If you're not making this aïoli to use in the Olive Oil–Poached Tuna Salad Sandwich (page 34), it can be made with plain olive oil and enjoyed as a spread on a sandwich that might need a pick-me-up. You could also dollop it on grilled fish or use it as a dip for French fries.

1 egg yolk (see box, page 309), at room temperature

1 teaspoon Dijon mustard

½ teaspoon salt

½ teaspoon finely grated orange zest

½ teaspoon finely grated lemon zest

1 tablespoon freshly squeezed orange juice

1 tablespoon freshly squeezed lemon juice

⅔ cup olive oil reserved from poached tuna (page 35) or plain olive oil

Combine the egg yolk, mustard, salt, orange and lemon zest, and orange and lemon juice in a small bowl. If necessary, secure the bowl to the work surface by setting a damp kitchen towel underneath. Slowly drizzle in the olive oil with one hand while whisking vigorously with the other to form an emulsion. Use immediately, or transfer to a small container, cover, and refrigerate for up to 3 days.

# HERBED AÏOLI

**1¼ cups**

What would this herb-a-licious mayonnaise *not* be good on? Toss it with romaine and Parmesan and cracked peppercorns, dollop it over a bowl of steamed mussels, mix it with boiled yolks for amazing deviled eggs, or add it to canned tuna for an easy tuna salad sandwich.

1 large egg (see box, page 309), at room temperature

1 tablespoon freshly squeezed lemon juice

1 teaspoon Dijon mustard

1 teaspoon minced garlic

½ teaspoon salt

¼ teaspoon freshly ground white pepper

1 teaspoon chopped fresh tarragon leaves

1 teaspoon chopped fresh chervil leaves

1 teaspoon snipped fresh chives

1 teaspoon chopped fresh parsley leaves

1 teaspoon chopped fresh basil leaves

1 cup olive oil

In the bowl of a food processor, combine the egg, lemon juice, mustard, garlic, salt, pepper, tarragon, chervil, chives, parsley, and basil. Process for 1 minute or until the herbs are pureed. While the motor is running, slowly add the olive oil in a thin, steady stream and blend until the mixture is thick. Use immediately or store, covered, in the refrigerator for up to 3 days.

# SPREADS, PESTOS, AND MUSTARDS

## BAGNA CAUDA DRIZZLE

**About 1 cup**

This is a versatile sauce that you'll enjoy serving with lots of things. If you happen to have any left over from the Fresh Tuna and Butter Lettuce Wraps (page 194), drizzle it over sliced tomatoes, roasted vegetables, or even pasta. The flavor improves as it sits, so for the best results, try to make this at least a day in advance.

| | |
|---|---|
| 1 cup extra-virgin olive oil | Salt, to taste |
| ¼ cup plus 1 tablespoon minced garlic | ¼ teaspoon freshly ground black pepper |
| 8 to 10 canned anchovy fillets, chopped | 2 pinches cayenne pepper |

1. Heat ¼ cup of the extra-virgin olive oil in a small saucepan over medium heat. When it is hot, add the garlic and cook until it is aromatic, about 1 minute. Add the remaining ¾ cup oil and the anchovies. Continue to cook over low heat until the anchovies dissolve, about 10 minutes.

2. Season the sauce with salt to taste; then add the black pepper and cayenne. Remove it from the heat and set it aside to cool.

3. Transfer the sauce to a blender, and puree. Use immediately, or place it in an airtight container and refrigerate until ready to serve; it will keep for several weeks. Return the sauce to room temperature before using.

**Sun-Dried Tomato**
**and Walnut Pesto**

**Bagna Cauda Drizzle**

**Mint Honey Mustard**

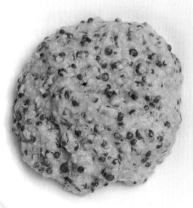

**Creole-Style Spicy**
**Mustard**

**Basil Spread**

# BASIL SPREAD

About ¾ cup

This basil spread is multifunctional. You can add it to store-bought mayonnaise, toss it with pasta, turn it into a vinaigrette, or add it to vegetable soups. And of course, it's fantastic on sandwiches.

1½ teaspoons minced garlic

1 cup packed fresh basil leaves

½ cup extra-virgin olive oil

½ teaspoon salt

In a food processor or blender, process the garlic and basil on high speed while adding the olive oil in a slow, steady stream. Continue to process until well blended. Season with the salt. Use immediately, or cover and refrigerate for up to 1 week.

# CREOLE-STYLE SPICY MUSTARD

2 cups

This mustard packs quite a punch, so watch out! Those of you who aren't as at home with spicy mustards might want to cut back a bit on the Colman's, because that's what gives this mustard a real kick. In New Orleans we just love our Creole mustard and use it on many things and in many sauces. It's similar to French or German whole-grain mustard, but it's definitely in a league of its own.

¼ cup plus 2 tablespoons brown mustard seeds

¼ cup yellow mustard seeds

1 tablespoon prepared horseradish

1 clove garlic, smashed

2½ teaspoons kosher salt, plus more if needed

½ cup plus 1 tablespoon white wine vinegar, plus more if needed

¼ cup plus 3 tablespoons dry white wine

¼ cup water

2 tablespoons Colman's dry mustard, or to taste

¾ teaspoon sugar

1. Combine the brown and yellow mustard seeds, horseradish, garlic, salt, vinegar, white wine, and water in a nonreactive bowl and stir to combine. Cover and refrigerate overnight.

2. The next day, stir in the dry mustard and the sugar (you may keep the garlic clove in or remove it at this point). Then transfer the mixture to a blender and puree until mostly smooth. (This type of mustard will never be completely smooth.) Transfer it to a nonreactive bowl and adjust the seasoning by adding more vinegar and/or salt if necessary. Refrigerate, covered, for up to 3 months.

## MINT HONEY MUSTARD

**About ½ cup**

Expand the kids' horizons: amazing on chicken tenders.

¼ cup chopped red onion

3 tablespoons whole-grain mustard

1 tablespoon honey

1½ tablespoons chopped fresh mint leaves

½ teaspoon finely grated lime zest

¼ teaspoon kosher salt

Stir all the ingredients together in a small bowl. Use immediately, or cover and refrigerate for up to 1 week.

Note: Should you desire to make more of this mustard, simply scale the amounts up proportionally.

# SUN-DRIED TOMATO AND WALNUT PESTO

**About 1½ cups**

As good as it is on the Three-Cheese Veggie Sandwich (page 36), this pesto can be used for lots of other things. Try it over pasta or tossed with vegetables, or throw a few spoonfuls of it into a bowl with salad fixings and use it as a dressing.

½ cup walnut halves or pieces, toasted

1 teaspoon minced garlic

½ cup fresh basil leaves

¼ cup fresh parsley leaves

¼ cup whole sun-dried tomatoes

¼ cup finely grated Parmigiano-Reggiano cheese

½ teaspoon salt

¼ teaspoon freshly ground black pepper

Finely grated zest of 1 lemon

1 teaspoon freshly squeezed lemon juice

1 tablespoon balsamic vinegar

½ cup extra-virgin olive oil

Place the walnuts in a food processor and pulse until they are thoroughly chopped. Add the garlic, basil, parsley, sun-dried tomatoes, Parmesan, salt, pepper, lemon zest, lemon juice, and balsamic vinegar. Pulse for a few seconds. With the machine running, add the oil in a steady stream to combine. Transfer the pesto to a serving bowl and use immediately, or cover and refrigerate for up to 1 week, or store in the freezer for 3 months.

# TAHINI AND YOGURT SAUCES

## TAHINI SAUCE

**About 2 cups**

Add several tablespoons of this sauce to a couple of cans drained chickpeas in the bowl of a food processor, pulse until smooth, and you have homemade hummus.

1 cup tahini paste

¼ cup plus 2 tablespoons freshly squeezed lemon juice, or more to taste

2 small cloves garlic, minced
    (about 1 teaspoon)

½ teaspoon salt

½ to ¾ cup water

In a medium bowl, whisk together the tahini paste, lemon juice, garlic, and salt. Add the water, a little at a time, as needed to form a smooth, creamy sauce that is about the consistency of heavy cream. (Note that the sauce might appear to separate a bit before enough water has been added; just keep adding more water bit by bit, stirring until the sauce comes together.) If necessary, season to taste with more salt and lemon juice. Cover and refrigerate until ready to use; it will keep for several weeks.

## RAITA

### About 2 cups

This very popular Indian condiment is awesome on the Smashed Chickpeas on Naan (page 170) and is also great with the samosas (see page 211) as a cooling dipping option.

2 cups peeled, seeded, and diced
    cucumber

¾ cup plain Greek-style yogurt

1 tablespoon freshly squeezed lime juice

¼ teaspoon finely grated lime zest

¼ teaspoon ground cumin

1 small fresh hot red chile, such as
    bird's-eye, Thai, or cayenne,
    stemmed, seeded, and minced

Salt, to taste

In a medium mixing bowl, combine the cucumber, yogurt, lime juice, lime zest, cumin, and chile. Season with salt to taste. Use immediately or cover and refrigerate until ready to use, up to 2 days.

## TZATZIKI SAUCE

### About 2¼ cups

This is delicious with the Beef Shawarma on page 179, but try it with warmed pita triangles and a simple tomato-onion salad for an easy appetizer, or with grilled lamb kebabs.

½ cup tahini paste

2 cloves garlic, smashed

¼ cup freshly squeezed lemon juice

¼ cup plain Greek-style yogurt

¼ cup extra-virgin olive oil

½ teaspoon salt

¼ teaspoon cayenne pepper

1 cup peeled, seeded, and diced cucumber

In a blender or a food processor, combine the tahini, garlic, lemon juice, yogurt, olive oil, salt, and cayenne. Puree for 30 seconds, or until all of the ingredients are well blended. Stir in the cucumber and use immediately, or cover and refrigerate for up to 2 days.

## SPICED YOGURT

About **3 cups**

Excellent not only on a falafel sandwich but also with fancy grilled lamb chops.

2 cups plain Greek-style yogurt

1 cup minced red onion

½ cup chopped fresh parsley leaves

½ cup chopped fresh mint leaves

2 tablespoons red wine vinegar

2 tablespoons extra-virgin olive oil

1 teaspoon finely grated orange zest

½ teaspoon ground sumac

¼ teaspoon cayenne pepper

1 teaspoon salt

In a medium mixing bowl, combine all the ingredients and mix well. Use immediately, or cover and refrigerate for up to 2 days.

# HARISSA, SALSA, AND OTHER HOT STUFF

## CLASSIC RED HARISSA

About **½ cup**

Though you certainly can purchase prepared harissa, I love the fresh, forward flavor of homemade. This is a perfect way to preserve the flavor of fresh chiles from your

Raita

Tahini Sauce

Spiced
Yogurt

Tzatziki Sauce

garden . . . and if you whip up a big batch, you can freeze it in small portions topped with a light film of olive oil to keep it fresh. I give instructions here for toasting whole cumin and caraway seeds and then grinding them for the freshest, most expressive flavor, but if you must, you can skip these steps and use freshly bought ground cumin and ground caraway.

1 tablespoon cumin seeds (see Notes)

1 tablespoon caraway seeds (see Notes)

4 ounces fresh red chiles, such as cayenne or red jalapeños, stems and seeds removed (see Notes)

4 cloves garlic, minced

½ teaspoon salt, plus more if needed

3 to 4 tablespoons extra-virgin olive oil, plus more for storing

1. Heat a small skillet over medium-high heat. Add the cumin seeds and cook, stirring or tossing them frequently, until they are aromatic, 30 seconds to 1 minute. Remove from the skillet and set aside to cool in a small bowl. Repeat with the caraway seeds, and set them aside to cool.

2. When the cumin seeds have cooled slightly, transfer them to a spice mill or a clean coffee grinder, and process until finely ground. Return the ground cumin to the small bowl and set aside. Repeat with the caraway seeds.

3. Measure 1½ teaspoons of the ground cumin and 1 teaspoon of the ground caraway, and combine in a mortar. (The remaining ground cumin and caraway can be used for other purposes.)

4. Place the chiles in the bowl of a food processor, and pulse until chopped. Add the chopped chiles, garlic, salt, and 1 tablespoon of the olive oil to the mortar. Using a pestle, mash repeatedly to form a chunky paste, adding more oil as needed to create a uniform texture. Taste, and adjust the seasoning if necessary by adding more salt or oil. Use immediately, or transfer the harissa to an airtight container, top it with a thin film of olive oil, and refrigerate for several weeks; or freeze in small batches for up to 6 months.

Green Harissa

Red Onion
and Tomato
Salsa Fresca

Classic Red Harissa

## Notes

- If you prefer, or if you don't have whole cumin or caraway seeds for step 1, simply skip that step and use 1½ teaspoons ground cumin and 1 teaspoon ground caraway, starting with step 3.

- I prefer the smooth texture of harissa when it is made without chile seeds, but if a rougher texture is desired, simply include the seeds. Be forewarned that the heat level will escalate, however!

# GREEN HARISSA

### About ¾ cup

The green chiles used here make for a milder harissa than the classic red version. Feel free to use different types of green chiles for variety—you'll see how different chiles provide a different heat level and flavor profile. I also love making this green version with roasted chiles; see the note at the end of the recipe.

1 tablespoon cumin seeds (see Notes)

1 tablespoon caraway seeds (see Notes)

4 ounces fresh hot green chiles, such as jalapeño or serrano, stems and seeds removed (see Notes)

4 ounces large mild green chiles, such as poblanos, long green chiles, New

Mexico chiles, or Anaheim chiles, stems and seeds removed (see Notes)

4 cloves garlic, minced

1 teaspoon kosher salt, plus more if needed

3 to 4 tablespoons extra-virgin olive oil, plus more for storing

1. Heat a small skillet over medium-high heat. Add the cumin seeds and cook, stirring or tossing them frequently, until they are aromatic, 30 seconds to 1 minute. Remove from the skillet and set aside to cool in a small bowl. Repeat with the caraway seeds and set them aside to cool.

2. When the cumin seeds have cooled slightly, transfer them to a spice mill or a clean coffee grinder, and process until finely ground. Return the ground cumin to the small bowl and set aside. Repeat with the caraway seeds.

3. Measure 1½ teaspoons of the ground cumin and 1 teaspoon of the ground caraway, and combine in a mortar. (The remaining ground cumin and caraway can be used for other purposes.)

4. Place all the green chiles in the bowl of a food processor, and pulse until finely chopped. Add the chopped chiles, garlic, salt, and 2 tablespoons of the olive oil to the mortar. Using a pestle, mash repeatedly to form a chunky paste, adding more oil as needed to form a uniform texture. Taste, and adjust the seasoning if necessary by adding more salt or oil. Use immediately, or transfer the harissa to an airtight container, top it with a thin film of olive oil, and refrigerate for several weeks; or freeze in small portions for up to 6 months.

### Notes

- If you prefer, or if you don't have whole cumin or caraway seeds for step 1, simply skip that step and use 1½ teaspoons ground cumin and 1 teaspoon ground caraway, starting with step 3.

- I prefer the smooth texture of harissa when it is made without chile seeds, but if a rougher texture is desired, simply include the seeds. Be forewarned that the heat level will escalate, however!

- Should you desire to make this with roasted chiles, simply toss the whole chiles with a tablespoon of vegetable oil to coat, and then roast them in a 450°F oven, turning them occasionally, until the skins are blistered and lightly charred, 25 to 30 minutes. Set aside to cool; then rub the skins off and discard them. Remove the stems and seeds, and chop the chiles finely. Stir in the remaining ingredients (the soft texture of the roasted chiles chops so nicely that there is no need for a mortar and pestle).

# RED ONION AND TOMATO SALSA FRESCA

**About 2¼ cups**

Of course it's great for chips and salsa, tacos, and quesadillas. But don't stop there—spoon it over grilled fish or even a burger.

3 medium-size ripe tomatoes, coarsely chopped (about 2 cups)

1 to 2 jalapeños, minced

¼ cup minced red onion

2 tablespoons freshly squeezed lime juice

1 clove garlic, minced

½ teaspoon kosher salt

⅓ cup coarsely chopped fresh cilantro leaves

1.  In a medium nonreactive bowl, combine the tomatoes, jalapeños, red onion, and lime juice.

2.  On a cutting board, mash the garlic and salt together, using the side of a chef's knife, to form a paste. Then add the garlic paste and the cilantro to the salsa, and stir to combine. Set aside briefly for the flavors to come together. Then serve with chips or as a topping for tacos, burritos, or quesadillas. This is best used the day it is made.

# VINAIGRETTES

## BALSAMIC-HERB VINAIGRETTE

¾ cup

Just add mixed greens and you're good to go!

¼ cup balsamic vinegar

1 tablespoon chopped fresh basil leaves

1 tablespoon chopped fresh oregano leaves

1 teaspoon minced garlic

½ cup extra-virgin olive oil

½ teaspoon salt

¼ teaspoon freshly ground black pepper

1. In a small mixing bowl, combine the balsamic vinegar, basil, oregano, and garlic; whisk well to mix. Continue whisking while slowly drizzling in the olive oil in a slow, steady stream. Add the salt and pepper, and whisk to combine.

2. The vinaigrette may be stored in an airtight container in the refrigerator for up to 1 week.

## DIJON VINAIGRETTE

1 cup

This classic French-style vinaigrette makes a great salad dressing and a terrific all-purpose marinade, and is wonderful drizzled over grilled vegetables or seafood. Note that the flavor will change dramatically based on the brands of mustard, vinegar, and olive oil you use. Experiment to find out which brands make you happy.

¼ cup red wine vinegar

¼ cup minced shallot

2 tablespoons whole-grain Dijon mustard

¼ teaspoon minced garlic

¼ teaspoon salt

⅛ teaspoon freshly ground black pepper

¼ cup olive oil

¼ cup extra-virgin olive oil

Fig Vinaigrette

Cranberry Vinaigrette

Dijon Vinaigrette

Balsamic-Herb Vinaigrette

1.  Combine the vinegar, shallot, mustard, garlic, salt, and pepper in a blender, and process for 45 seconds. While the blender is still running, slowly add the olive oils in a thin, steady stream, processing until the vinaigrette is emulsified.

2.  The vinaigrette can be stored in a nonreactive airtight container in the refrigerator for up to 1 week.

## CRANBERRY VINAIGRETTE

### Scant 1 cup

Pour this into a large resealable plastic food storage bag and add a pork tenderloin to marinate while you're at work. Grill or roast it when you get home for a fantastic dinner. Great served with the Cranberry Chutney on page 340.

2 tablespoons cider vinegar

2 tablespoons cranberry juice, preferably unsweetened

2 tablespoons chopped dried cranberries

1 teaspoon Dijon mustard

½ cup grapeseed oil

½ teaspoon salt

¼ teaspoon freshly ground black pepper

1.  In a small bowl, combine the vinegar, cranberry juice, dried cranberries, and Dijon mustard. While whisking, add the grapeseed oil in a thin, steady stream until completely incorporated and emulsified. Whisk in the salt and pepper.

2.  The vinaigrette can be stored in an airtight container in the refrigerator for up to 1 week.

## FIG VINAIGRETTE

**About ½ cup**

Drizzle this over the blue cheese wedge on your cheese plate and your guests will go wild.

¼ cup fig preserves (chopped if figs are whole)

2 tablespoons balsamic vinegar

¼ cup grapeseed oil

Pinch of salt and freshly ground black pepper

1. In a small bowl, combine the fig preserves and vinegar. Whisk in the grapeseed oil, and season with a pinch of salt and pepper.

2. The vinaigrette will keep, refrigerated in an airtight nonreactive container, for up to 2 weeks.

# RÉMOULADES AND CREAMY DRESSINGS

## AVOCADO CREMA

**About 1¾ cups**

Though terrific on the Breakfast Burrito (page 229), this works great as a delicious dip too—happily eaten with the humble tortilla chip, dolloped on tacos, or even spread on sandwiches.

2 ripe avocados, halved, pitted, and scooped from peel

½ cup Mexican crema, sour cream, or crème fraîche

2 tablespoons freshly squeezed lime juice

1 tablespoon finely chopped fresh cilantro leaves

1 teaspoon salt

¼ teaspoon chipotle chile powder

⅛ teaspoon ancho chile powder

⅛ teaspoon ground cumin

⅛ teaspoon cayenne pepper

1.  Combine all the ingredients in the bowl of a food processor and process until smooth, scraping down the sides of the bowl as necessary.

2.  Transfer to a bowl and serve immediately, or place a piece of plastic wrap directly on top of the crema and refrigerate it for up to 1 week.

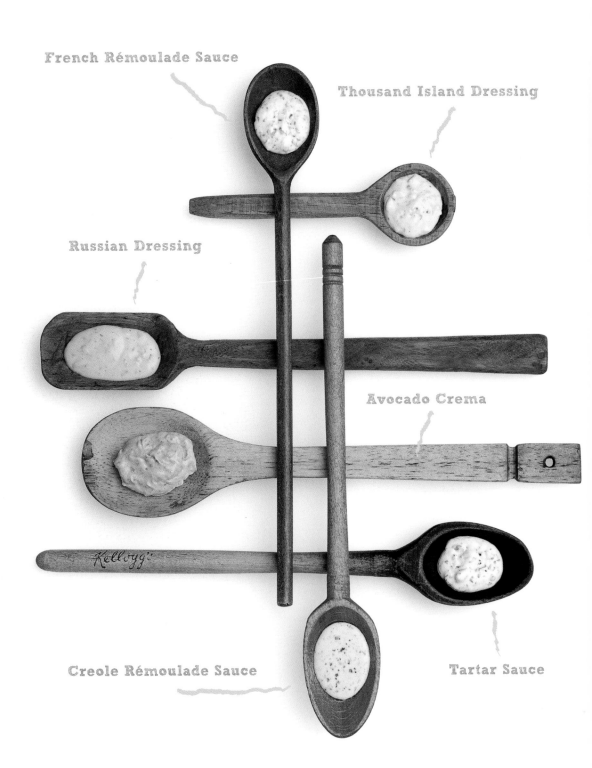

French Rémoulade Sauce

Thousand Island Dressing

Russian Dressing

Avocado Crema

Creole Rémoulade Sauce

Tartar Sauce

# CREOLE RÉMOULADE SAUCE

**About 2½ cups**

This version of rémoulade is the one you'll find most often in New Orleans—it is ever so slightly pink from the hint of ketchup and has a little kick from the horseradish and cayenne. It's delicious with seafood and is a classic showstopper.

1 large egg yolk (see box, page 309), at room temperature

¼ cup Creole mustard (preferably Zatarain's) or Creole-Style Spicy Mustard (page 318)

2½ tablespoons red wine vinegar

1 tablespoon prepared horseradish

1 teaspoon kosher salt

1 teaspoon paprika

½ teaspoon cayenne pepper

¼ teaspoon freshly ground black pepper

1 clove garlic, minced

¾ cup vegetable oil

¼ cup olive oil

½ cup finely minced celery

¼ cup plus 2 tablespoons minced green onion

¼ cup mayonnaise, homemade (see page 309), or store-bought

1 tablespoon ketchup, homemade (see page 339), or store-bought

¼ teaspoon Worcestershire sauce

1.  In a nonreactive mixing bowl, whisk together the egg yolk, mustard, vinegar, horseradish, ¾ teaspoon of the salt, the paprika, cayenne, and black pepper. On a cutting board, mash the garlic and the remaining ¼ teaspoon salt together, using the side of a chef's knife, to form a paste. Add the garlic paste to the bowl and whisk to combine.

2.  Combine the oils in a measuring cup with a pour spout, and while whisking continuously, drizzle the oil blend very slowly into the mustard mixture until a smooth, thick emulsion is formed. Whisk in the celery, green onion, mayonnaise, ketchup, and Worcestershire sauce. Chill thoroughly before using; the rémoulade will keep for up to 2 days in the refrigerator.

# FRENCH RÉMOULADE SAUCE

**1 generous cup**

This classic French sauce differs from its Creole cousin in that it contains no tomato element. It actually more closely resembles our American tartar sauce . . . but like its Creole counterpart, it too is delicious with seafood in all guises.

1 cup mayonnaise, homemade (see page 309), or store-bought

2 tablespoons chopped fresh parsley leaves

1 tablespoon chopped fresh chives

1 tablespoon freshly squeezed lemon juice

1 tablespoon minced shallot

1 teaspoon Dijon mustard

1 teaspoon chopped capers

1 teaspoon chopped cornichon

1 teaspoon minced garlic

1 teaspoon chopped fresh tarragon leaves

1 canned anchovy fillet, minced

½ teaspoon finely grated lemon zest

¼ teaspoon sea salt

⅛ teaspoon freshly ground black pepper

⅛ teaspoon cayenne pepper

Combine all the ingredients in a medium bowl and stir to combine. Chill thoroughly before using. The rémoulade will keep for up to 2 days in the refrigerator.

# RUSSIAN DRESSING

**About 1½ cups**

A classic you make fresh!

1 cup mayonnaise, homemade (see page 309), or store-bought

½ cup chili sauce

1 tablespoon minced dill pickle

1 tablespoon minced celery

1 tablespoon minced fresh parsley leaves

1 tablespoon heavy cream

½ teaspoon dry mustard

½ teaspoon hot sauce, such as Tabasco    ¼ teaspoon sugar

¼ teaspoon Worcestershire sauce

In a bowl, combine all the ingredients and whisk until well blended. Cover and refrigerate until ready to serve. The dressing will keep for 3 days in the refrigerator.

## TARTAR SAUCE

About 2 cups

Fry up catfish fillets or shrimp and have a field day.

1½ cups mayonnaise, homemade (see page 309), or store-bought

2 tablespoons minced red onion

2 tablespoons finely chopped cornichons

1 tablespoon finely chopped capers

1 tablespoon minced shallot

1 tablespoon minced garlic

1 tablespoon chopped fresh parsley leaves

1 tablespoon chopped fresh tarragon leaves

2 tablespoons freshly squeezed lemon juice

½ teaspoon salt

¼ teaspoon freshly ground white pepper

Combine all the ingredients in a medium mixing bowl and stir to combine. Cover and refrigerate the tartar sauce for at least 1 hour to allow the flavors to come together before using. The sauce can be made up to 3 days in advance.

# THOUSAND ISLAND DRESSING

**About 2 cups**

Not what you'll find on that fast-food burger . . .

1 egg yolk (see box, page 309), at room
temperature

1 tablespoon freshly squeezed lemon
juice

¼ cup minced onion

¼ cup chopped green olives

1 hard-boiled egg, finely chopped

1 tablespoon sweet pickle relish

1 tablespoon chopped pimento

1 tablespoon chopped fresh chives

1 tablespoon chili sauce

1 teaspoon minced garlic

¾ teaspoon salt

¼ teaspoon freshly ground black pepper

1 cup vegetable oil

In a medium bowl, whisk together the egg yolk and the lemon juice. Add the
onion, olives, chopped egg, relish, pimentos, chives, chili sauce, garlic, salt, and
pepper. Slowly whisk in the oil to form an emulsion. Use immediately, or cover and
refrigerate for up to 1 week.

# KETCHUPS, CHUTNEYS, AND JAM

## SPICY HOMEMADE KETCHUP

### 2½ cups

I couldn't have a condiment chapter without ketchup. This one is killer.

2 tablespoons vegetable oil

1 cup chopped red onion

1 tablespoon minced fresh ginger

2 teaspoons minced garlic

1 teaspoon crushed red pepper

1¾ teaspoons kosher salt

½ teaspoon ground mustard

¼ teaspoon ground mace

⅛ teaspoon ground allspice

⅛ teaspoon ground cloves

¼ cup cider vinegar

¼ cup packed light brown sugar

¼ cup raisins

One 28-ounce can whole tomatoes, with juices, crushed with your hands

¼ cup water

1 tablespoon malt vinegar

1 teaspoon balsamic vinegar

1.  Heat a medium saucepan over medium-high heat. When it is hot, add the vegetable oil, onion, ginger, garlic, and crushed red pepper. Cook until the vegetables have softened, 4 to 5 minutes.

2.  Add the salt, mustard, mace, allspice, and cloves, and cook, stirring, until fragrant, 1 to 2 minutes. Add the vinegar, brown sugar, and raisins, and cook until the vinegar has thickened, about 2 minutes. Add the tomatoes, their juices, and the water, and bring to a boil. Reduce the heat to medium-low and simmer until the mixture has thickened and the flavors have come together, 25 to 30 minutes.

3.  Remove the pan from the heat and allow to cool briefly. Transfer the mixture to a blender and process until it is very smooth. Add the malt vinegar and balsamic vinegar, and stir to combine. Serve at room temperature or slightly chilled.

4.  Store the ketchup, covered, in a nonreactive container in the refrigerator for up to 3 weeks.

## CILANTRO-MINT CHUTNEY

Generous ¾ cup

Should you happen to have any of this left over from the chickpea sandwiches on page 170, it makes an awesome marinade for chicken.

1 cup packed fresh cilantro leaves

½ cup packed fresh mint leaves

2 jalapeños, stemmed, seeded, and chopped

1 tablespoon freshly squeezed lemon juice

½ cup unsweetened coconut milk

½ teaspoon palm sugar or light brown sugar

½ teaspoon salt

1.  In a blender, combine the cilantro, mint, jalapeños, lemon juice, and just enough water to allow the ingredients to process; blend until smooth.

2.  In a small mixing bowl, combine the coconut milk, palm sugar, salt, and cilantro-mint mixture. Mix well and set the chutney aside, covered, until ready to use; or refrigerate it for up to 2 days.

## CRANBERRY CHUTNEY

1 quart

Cranberry chutney is a great thing to have on hand, not only because it is a great condiment for sandwiches but also because you can serve it with roast pork and poultry. Or try it on a cheese plate with a hard cheese such as Manchego, or even with a soft, creamy goat's-milk cheese.

1 pound fresh or frozen cranberries

½ cup small-diced red onion

½ cup packed light brown sugar

½ cup apple juice

½ cup cider vinegar

¼ cup cranberry juice, preferably unsweetened

½ teaspoon dry mustard

½ teaspoon ground ginger

¼ teaspoon ground allspice

Cranberry
Chutney

Tamarind
Sauce

Kansas
City–Style
Barbecue
Sauce

Cilantro-Mint
Chutney

Tamarind
Chutney

Onion Jam

Homemade
Spicy
Ketchup

¼ teaspoon ground cardamom

¼ teaspoon ground cinnamon

¼ teaspoon crushed red pepper

⅛ teaspoon salt

1 Honeycrisp apple, unpeeled, cored and diced small, or other sweet, crisp apple

1.  In a medium nonreactive saucepan, combine the cranberries, red onion, brown sugar, apple juice, cider vinegar, cranberry juice, mustard, ginger, allspice, cardamom, cinnamon, crushed red pepper, and salt. Cook for 20 minutes over medium heat, or until the cranberries begin to pop.

2.  Add the apple and cook for another 10 to 15 minutes, until the mixture thickens enough to coat the back of a spoon (the mixture will continue to thicken as it cools).

3.  Let the chutney cool, and store it, covered, in the refrigerator for up to 1 month.

## KANSAS CITY–STYLE BARBECUE SAUCE

**About 2 cups**

This tangy middle-of-the-road barbecue sauce isn't too spicy or too sweet—it's just right. Use it any time a barbecue urge beckons. I love it on pulled pork, and slathered over barbecued chicken or ribs.

1 cup store-bought ketchup

½ cup cider vinegar

3 tablespoons dark brown sugar

1 tablespoon plus 1 teaspoon Worcestershire sauce

1 tablespoon cane syrup or dark corn syrup

2 teaspoons chopped garlic

½ teaspoon finely grated onion

½ teaspoon salt

¼ teaspoon freshly ground black pepper

¼ teaspoon ground ginger

¼ teaspoon ground allspice

¼ teaspoon dry mustard

¼ teaspoon cayenne pepper

Combine all the ingredients in a blender, and process until thoroughly blended and smooth. The sauce can be made up to 1 week in advance and refrigerated in an airtight nonreactive container.

## ONION JAM

**1 cup**

Not only is this jam great on burgers, it is perfect served alongside grilled or roasted meats or as an addition to a cheese and charcuterie plate.

2 tablespoons olive oil

2 tablespoons unsalted butter

4 cups thinly sliced red onion

½ cup apple cider

½ cup cider vinegar

¼ cup sugar

1 sprig fresh rosemary

¼ teaspoon sea salt

¼ teaspoon freshly ground black pepper

1.   Heat the olive oil and butter in a medium heavy-bottomed nonreactive saucepan over medium heat. When it is hot, add the onion and cook for about 15 minutes, stirring as needed, until it is caramelized.

2.   Add the apple cider, vinegar, sugar, rosemary sprig, salt, and pepper. Reduce the heat to medium-low and cook for another 30 to 35 minutes, stirring occasionally, until the onion has reached a jamlike consistency.

3.   Discard the rosemary sprig and set the jam aside to cool before using, or cover and refrigerate for up to 1 week.

# TAMARIND CHUTNEY

Generous 2 cups

This sweet-and-sour dipping sauce is more on the thick side than the Tamarind Sauce on page 345. It's the perfect complement to the samosas on page 211. The chutney is pure tamarind reconstituted and mixed with sugar and spice. An authentic take.

8 ounces tamarind pulp (see Note), cut into 8 chunks

2 cups boiling water

½ cup packed light brown sugar

½ teaspoon garam masala

½ teaspoon salt

⅛ teaspoon cayenne pepper

2 tablespoons water, if needed

1.   Place the tamarind in a small bowl and pour the boiling water over it. Cover and set aside until softened, 15 to 20 minutes.

2.   Mash and squeeze the tamarind (with gloved hands—it will be warm and quite sticky) to separate the seeds and skin from the pulp. Strain the pulp through a metal colander, or through a fine-mesh sieve, set over another small bowl. Discard the solids. Stir in the brown sugar, garam masala, salt, and cayenne, and set aside to cool. If the chutney is too thick, thin it with up to 2 tablespoons water. Store it, covered, in the refrigerator for up to 1 month.

Note: Tamarind pulp is available in Middle Eastern and Asian markets and is sold in blocks wrapped in plastic. It's the entire tamarind fruit, seeds and all, and thus needs to be loosened in warm water and then put through a strainer before it can be used. It should not be confused with tamarind concentrate, which is a completely different product that is spoonable and already strained. They should not be used interchangeably in recipes.

# TAMARIND SAUCE

**1 cup**

This fantastic sauce is a blend of coconut milk, tamarind concentrate, and of course sugar and spice. Its sweet and tangy complexion is wonderful drizzled on the Thai-Style Grilled Curried Chicken wrap on page 189.

1 tablespoon vegetable oil

½ cup minced shallot

1 tablespoon minced garlic

1 tablespoon minced fresh ginger

1 to 2 fresh hot chiles, such as Thai, bird's-eye, cayenne, or red jalapeño, stemmed, seeded, and finely chopped

½ cup tamarind concentrate, such as Tamicon brand (see page 344)

½ cup unsweetened coconut milk

3 tablespoons palm sugar or light brown sugar, plus more if needed

2 tablespoons fish sauce, plus more if needed

1 cup water

1.  Heat the vegetable oil in a medium saucepan over medium-high heat. Add the shallot, garlic, ginger, and chiles, and sauté, stirring constantly, until fragrant, about 1 minute.

2.  Add the tamarind, coconut milk, sugar, fish sauce, and water. Whisk together to combine, and then bring to a boil over medium-high heat. Reduce the heat to a brisk simmer and cook until the sauce thickens and the flavors come together, about 6 minutes.

3.  Remove the pan from the heat and adjust the flavor with more fish sauce and/or sugar to taste. Transfer the mixture to a blender, and puree. Set the sauce aside until ready to use, or refrigerate, covered, for up to 1 month. Serve at room temperature.

# BÉARNAISE SAUCE

## BÉARNAISE SAUCE

**About 1½ cups**

Hollandaise is one of the five Mother Sauces, and béarnaise is simply hollandaise with tarragon. If you want to have a special evening, it's exceptional over roasted asparagus, Brussels sprouts, and filet mignon.

¼ cup white wine vinegar

¼ cup good-quality dry white wine

2 tablespoons minced shallot

2 sprigs fresh tarragon, plus 2 tablespoons chopped fresh tarragon leaves

6 to 8 white peppercorns

3 egg yolks (see box, page 309)

1 cup (2 sticks) unsalted butter, melted

¼ teaspoon kosher salt

1.   Place the vinegar, white wine, shallot, tarragon sprigs, and white peppercorns in a small saucepan and bring to a boil over medium-high heat. Immediately reduce the heat to medium and simmer until the mixture has reduced to 3 tablespoons. Strain through a fine-mesh sieve. Discard the solids.

2.   Add the egg yolks and the strained vinegar reduction to a blender, and process for 30 seconds. While the blender is still running, add the butter in a thin, slow stream; the sauce should become fairly thick. Add the chopped tarragon and the salt, and blend for another 30 seconds. Use the béarnaise sauce immediately or as soon as possible. If it becomes too thick, add 1 or 2 teaspoons of hot water and stir well.

# INDEX

Note: Page references in *italics* indicate photographs.